Praise for *Supercharged Te*

C000281781

'*Supercharged Teams* understands the power of a team motivated by purpose to do work that has impact beyond the bottom line, and offers the tools to help your team to deliver results that pay a human dividend. It's a must-read for all leaders who want to make a transformative difference.'

Syl Saller CBE, Chief Marketing and Innovation Officer, Diageo

'Packed with questions to ask yourself, examples and lessons learned from a wide range of experts, this book is an indispensable guide for anyone who wants their team to perform better.'

Ben Page, Chief Executive, Ipsos MORI

'*Supercharged Teams* is a go-to practical book to get teams to perform at their best. An easy and involving read with case studies, reflections and tools to improve team collaboration, effectiveness and joy.

There is nothing more frustrating than sitting in a room with people that are not engaged, or distracted or multi-tasking. Still, this is a common complaint we hear so often. With plenty of thought-provoking questions, *Supercharged Teams* makes you re-evaluate how well you are working as a team, covering a wide spectrum of topics for great teamwork – from choosing the right team, to building a team culture.

As an experienced leader I have had the privilege to be part and lead numerous teams – the extraordinary, the good, the ugly. Great teamwork doesn't happen overnight, and it requires a constant and conscious effort to establish the right dynamics, behaviours, ways of working and culture. Making time to reflect and implement specific practices can make a gigantic and immediate difference. Reading the book inspired me straightway to try different approaches and shake the teams I am currently working. The difference was noticeable and sincerely appreciated.

Whether you are a member of a team or a talented leader, *Supercharged Teams* can support you to take your collaboration and performance to the next level. A 5-star rating.'

Ricardo Arantes, Global Brand Director, Unilever

'When I think about why I work and when I get the most satisfaction out of work, being part of a high functioning team is at the heart. In this book, Pam Hamilton, through a beautifully narrated story, provides tools for how to team effectively. She expertly takes into consideration the current and future challenges facing the workforce. Striving for more diversity? A super-charged team is a critical strategy. The concepts here are at the same time fundamental, foundational and game-changing.'

Beth Ann Kaminkow, Global CEO, Geometry

'Our disrupted, complex business world demands agility. The problem: much organisational "teamwork" is unworthy of the name. Pam Hamilton offers you a practical, accessible and motivating toolkit to supercharge your team. Let's get to work!'

Greg Orme, author of the award-winning *The Human Edge*

'Insightful and highly relevant in today's changing world of work, *Supercharged Teams* provides thirty practical tools to increase your productivity and performance. With distributed and virtual working quickly becoming the way we now operate, Pam's book is essential reading for all team leaders and players who want to be more effective at achieving purposeful work.'

Natalie Turner, author, of *Yes, You Can Innovate*

'Pam knows how to supercharge your teams and, now more than ever, we do need supercharged teams!'

Gael De Talhouet, VP Brand Building, Global Brands, Innovations and Sustainability, Essity

'This straightforward approach to sharing information is refreshing – short, sharp snapshots that outline a concept, then expand on it with stories and case studies, so you can choose to skim through or go into detail, depending on your need. Lots of great ideas and snippets – I loved the suggestion to deliberately and consciously agree on the mindset, pace and approach for a team, and I'm looking forward to trying out the "reframe your aim" exercise on my next project.'

Katherine Richards, HR Director, Arnott's Biscuits

'What teamwork looks like is changing fast. You can either try to figure it out on your own, or take on Pamela Hamilton's expert advice, gained from building and facilitating high-performing teams around the world. 'Supercharged Teams: 30 Tools of Great Teamwork' offers method, structure, and strategies for self-awareness which I have already started to share with my clients.'

Remy Blumenfeld, Forbes Contributor and Founder, Vitality.Guru

'In my role as Pitch Director, my team lead innovation workshops and so it is vital they work together as an effective team and are able to drive collaboration amongst the project groups they work with. I found this book genuinely interesting, thought-provoking and filled with examples and tools which leaders can put instantly into action.'

Emma Wingate, Pitch Global Innovation Director, Unilever

'Pam knows what she is talking about. She has seen so many teams up close and knows what makes them tick – or stink. There is a kind of genius in her ability to analyse complex human interactions and create potent tools that really work. And she has the most wonderfully contagious laugh…'

Neil Mullarkey, author, coach, and improviser with the Comedy Store Players

'Whether you are a new or well-established team, I would thoroughly recommend *Supercharged Teams*. It is packed with practical advice, tools and exercises to enhance the performance, ways of working and culture of your team.

This is not a "fluffy" management book to read and consign to the bookshelf, it is one to be used again and again.'

Helen Wing, Head of Innovation, Ipsos Mori

'Full of "aha!" moments that explain why teams I've been in have been dysfunctional – and plenty of really practical tools that will remind me how to channel Pam when I'm in them in future!'

Clare Thompson, Media Trends and
Non-Executive Director, K7 Media

'Our world might have changed as a result of the coronavirus, but the need to work together to solve our challenges most certainly hasn't. This book is exactly what leaders need right now: an accessible and practical book that delivers instant positive returns. Your team – and what you can do together – will be transformed by it!'

Henry Mason, Evangelist-at-large, TrendWatching;
Co-founder, 3Space

'If the rapidly accelerating pace and demands of life and work get on top of you from time to time then this book is an absolute godsend! Never has the human side of business mattered so much, especially as technology, remote working accelerates – we need each other more than ever. In this book Pam lays out exactly why being part of a supercharged team is so important, not just for success but also to feel great at work. Her tips and techniques are inspiring, easy to apply and a great reference to dip into whatever your need.'

Wendy Adams, Global CMI Director, Unilever Ice Cream

'If I had been able to read this book 30 years ago how different my work life would have been. Every manager needs to read this book and then share it with their team. Every organisation needs multiple copies in their library, canteen and reception areas. It's straightforward, wise and very readable. Miss it at your peril.'

Irene Grindell, Professional Accredited Mediator and
Conflict Coach, Irene Grindell Resolutions Consultancy Ltd

'*Supercharged Teams* is an invaluable, and timely, resource for those looking to get the best out of their teams in an ever-changing world. Packed with detailed case studies, and essential, practical, and actionable tips and tools this is a book for any leader of teams, in any industry, in any country.'

Bruce Robertson, Executive Producer, Non-Scripted TV, USA

'Having had the great pleasure to work with Pam, I know first-hand what a wonderful combination of professional excellence and clarity combined with human warmth and empathy Pam embodies. She is extremely skilled at articulating the most relevant topics with precision and brevity while allowing others to buy-in and feel understood and supported.

Being a passionate believer in teams myself since I was a little boy, I particularly like Pam's core belief articulated throughout the entire book that – if designed and delivered well aligned – teamwork empowers healthy high performance. It moves mountains and can create goose bumps moments of joy by achieving success that team members themselves deemed impossible at the beginning.

Yes, as articulated in chapter 2, not all work requires a team and yes, teamwork needs and is hard work. However, the vast majority of results in the world today are achieved better, faster or at lower cost if created by a team. And with further increasing volatility, uncertainty, complexity, and ambiguity, in the future good teamwork will become even more crucial than ever before.

Finally, I love the excellent balance Pam strikes in marrying relevant, insightful, intellectually sound theory with valuable real-world practice and case studies. The book's structure and the 30 tools enable the reader to turn insight into action.

No matter if you are a first-time leader or CEO, *Supercharged Teams* is a pleasure and must-read for any leader. Thank you, Pam, for giving us this wonderful, insightful and inspiring guide to do one of the most important and fun bits of our jobs today – leading teams to success.'

**Stefan Homeister, Founder and Owner,
Stefan Homeister Leadership GmbH**

'My copy of Pamela's last book is dog-eared, decorated with little post-it tags and almost never makes it back onto the shelf. I expect *Supercharged Teams* will go the same way. It's a roadmap for anyone who wants to lead purposeful and productive teams: a usable framework, relatable examples and dozens of practical tools.'

Mike Stevens, Founder, Insight Platforms

'*Supercharged Teams* is a one-stop shop for any leader or facilitator who wants support in getting their teams to the next level. The book is bursting with practical advice, tools and templates to make anyone feel confident when getting people to enhance their collaboration skills. This is the type of book that you will return to again and again for sage advice when you need it most. It's a must for all leaders and anyone who genuinely cares about enhancing their team's performance.'

**Jodie Rogers, Leadership and
Professional Development expert**

'Intuitively we know being part of a team is better than working alone therefore we instinctively pull a team of people around us to work on projects and to be together.

Yet creating a team that understand one another, work effectively together and achieve their goals is another layer of complexity for leaders and managers in the modern world.

What Pam Hamilton has achieved with this book is a way for you to work out why you need a team, how you create THE best team for the job AND THEN she has only gone and given us a step-by-step guide packed with 20+ different meeting frameworks, exercises and ways of working to ensure this team, virtual or in-person, is awesome and achieving what they set out to do.'

Kirsty Lewis, Founder, School of Facilitation

'*Supercharged Teams* brings you all the support you need for quality teamwork that runs on time, meets objectives, and delivers outcomes that the team is proud of and the business values.

Never once forgetting that the team operates within a wider culture, the book is teeming with tips, tools and real-life case studies in this well-researched exploration of barriers to effective teamwork and the practical tools to address them.

Grounded in the reality of business now and in the future, Pam Hamilton reminds us that supercharged teams don't stand still. They evolve project by project and over time. As team members and leaders her guidance and practical tools will help you ensure you are always up to date, relevant and supercharged in your teamwork.'

Lyn Roseaman, Founder and Public Speaking Coach,
Now You're Talking

'Pam's passion and personality comes through on every page making you want to know more ... easy to read, full of great tips and light bulb moments.'

Louise Wilders, CEO, The HIVE Portsmouth

'The numerous practical tools are designed to spark high-value conversations, according to the priorities of the team and the teams' wider stakeholders. Teams at different stages of their teaming journey will find targeted tools to shine the spotlight, i.e. To evaluate team purpose, membership, and momentum; the effectiveness of true collaboration; habits of relentless prioritisation and tools for building teamship. In addition to the tools, Pam includes a broad selection of case studies and shares her valuable experience in the field which gives context. This book will be of interest to anyone aiming to increase their chances of success, to sharpen their own performance and the performance of the team.'

Sue Gravells, Life-long learner as a Leader of Teams,
Team Member and Team Coach

Supercharged Teams

Pearson

At Pearson, we have a simple mission: to help people make more of their lives through learning.

We combine innovative learning technology with trusted content and educational expertise to provide engaging and effective learning experiences that serve people wherever and whenever they are learning.

From classroom to boardroom, our curriculum materials, digital learning tools and testing programmes help to educate millions of people worldwide – more than any other private enterprise.

Every day our work helps learning flourish, and wherever learning flourishes, so do people.

To learn more, please visit us at **www.pearson.com/uk**

Supercharged Teams

The 30 Tools of Great Teamwork

Pamela Hamilton

Foreword by Michael Schrage

Pearson

Harlow, England • London • New York • Boston • San Francisco • Toronto • Sydney • Dubai • Singapore • Hong Kong
Tokyo • Seoul • Taipei • New Delhi • Cape Town • São Paulo • Mexico City • Madrid • Amsterdam • Munich • Paris • Milan

PEARSON EDUCATION LIMITED
KAO Two
KAO Park
Harlow CM17 9SR
United Kingdom
Tel: +44 (0)1279 623623
Web: www.pearson.com/uk

First edition published 2021 (print and electronic)

ISBN: 978-1-292-33464-6 (print)
         978-1-292-33465-3 (PDF)
         978-1-292-33466-0 (ePub)

British Library Cataloguing-in-Publication Data
A catalogue record for the print edition is available from the British Library

Library of Congress Cataloging-in-Publication Data
A catalog record for the print edition is available from the Library of Congress

10 9 8 7 6 5 4 3
25 24 23 22 21

Cover design by Madras

Print edition typeset in 10/14 Charter ITC Pro by SPi Global
Printed by Ashford Colour Press Ltd, Gosport

NOTE THAT ANY PAGE CROSS REFERENCES REFER TO THE PRINT EDITION

Contents

Contents

About the author

—

Pamela Hamilton is a teamwork and collaboration expert, with over 20 years' experience working with global and local businesses, teams, communities and people to help them work better together. With a background in psychology, and a passion for collective intelligence, Pam works to empower people, develop their capabilities and facilitate positive change.

Pam is the author of *The Workshop Book* and has developed 'Project Bridge', a public sector co-creation method to bring communities together to solve complex issues. As the founder of global agency Paraffin, she designs and leads bespoke insight, innovation and capability journeys for consumer goods, financial services, public sector and media clients.

With *Supercharged Teams*, Pam provides you with the tools and approaches you need to reset any team to work together successfully. Visit www.superchargedteams.com for more information, free downloads, templates, case studies and further training available to anyone who has bought this book.

Acknowledgements

———

After *The Workshop Book,* I knew I wanted to write a book on collaboration, and I have been collecting case studies and research on the topic for years. It took me a while (and excellent advice from Eloise Cook, my editor) to establish that the book I wanted to write was about incredible teamwork, the kind that incorporates collaboration, creativity, purpose, energy and momentum. This led to *Supercharged Teams.*

Many busy, talented and clever people have chosen to give me their time, ideas and support in writing this book. These are people who have their own projects to complete, teams to run, businesses to lead, families to support and books to write. This book was completed during the global COVID-19 pandemic, which makes the support I received even more incredible, as they all gave me their time while navigating a crisis. I cannot thank them enough for their generosity of spirit and their commitment to collaborating with me.

Thank you especially to Malcolm D'Sa, who, when I was ready to give up on writing a second book, kept urging me on; Beth Ann Kaminkow, for her kind support and positive influence; Grainne Wafer who exemplifies the authentic and purpose-driven leader I would like to be; Gael De Talhouet who provoked and challenged my ideas; and Laura Diamond whose analysis and expertise refined my thinking. I was honoured to be mentored by the brilliant Michael

Schrage, whose incisive challenges and fast feedback sharpened and strengthened my work. His advice to put more of myself into the book made it so much more enjoyable to write and, I hope, to read.

I would like to thank the people who made this book possible by giving me the space and time to write: Alison Darling, who runs our business and our teams so brilliantly; Anna Johnson, who inspires and creates incredible content; Anne Nørholm Iverson, with her design eye and systems thinking; Dee O'Brien who protected and organised my time; and Nicola Waterman, my clever and talented writing partner who has helped me to turn a pile of Post-its, flipcharts, research and dictations into a fully written book. Thank you to the Paraffin team, the brain of brains who helped me to create the title of the book and gave me case studies, ideas, examples and inspiration whenever I got stuck.

Thank you to the people who went above and beyond to help me with ideas, interviews and advice, including Sofia Mavros, Emma Wingate, Sue Phillips, Andrea Wareham, Ben Page, Monica Juanas, Jennifer Whyte, Steve Pitt, Marcus Cator, Irene Grindell, Rachel Green, Neil Mullarkey, Clare Thompson, Amber D'Albert, Brooke Hoskins, Stefan Homeister, Henry Mason, Carl Hartman and Claire Emes.

And thank you to everyone who contributed so kindly, including Wendy Aitken, Penny Bennett, Adrian Bleasdale, Markay Bressler, Graham Charles, Pele Cortizo-Burgess, Richard Evans, Brady Grange, Rhia Harry, Caroline Haworth, Craige Heaney, 'Julia Hobsbawm, Katie Hyams, Billie Ing, Shalaka Karandikar, Briana Larkin, Michelle Lavipour, Coral McConnon, Claudia Nielsen, Catherine Mangan, Henry Mason, John Monks, Rob Myles, Greg Orme, Sarah Peachey, Bruce Robertson, Ian Roe, Syl Saller, Patrizia Sorgiovanni, Guy Stevens, Marie Stopforth, Ian Thwaites, Richard Watkins, Rachel Webley, Ben White and Louise Wilders.

Thank you to The HIVE Portsmouth, Portsmouth City Council and Portsmouth Guildhall, who have welcomed me into the community and have taught me so much.

And finally a deep thank you to Paul Bennett, my husband, for being my hero, navigator and advisor; Min Wright, for her kindness and constant support; Tamlyn Norcott and Katherine Richards for their endless belief in me; Ian Wright who taught me never to accept what I could change for the better; and my daughter Bailey for her energy and spirit, and whose generation will work together in better ways than we can ever imagine today.

Publisher's acknowledgements

1 **Helen Keller:** Quoted by Helen Keller 3 **Steve Jobs:** Quoted by Steve Jobs 5 **J. Richard Hackman:** Quoted by J. Richard Hackman 8 **Reid Hoffman:** Quoted by Reid Hoffman 17 **Sir Barnett Cocks:** Quoted by Sir Barnett Cocks 18 **Gael De Talhouet:** Quoted by Gael De Talhouet 21 **J. Richard Hackman:** Quoted by J. Richard Hackman 23 **Greg Orme:** Quoted by Greg Orme 23 **Julian Baggini:** Quoted by Julian Baggini 30 **Steve Jobs:** Quoted by Steve Jobs 31 **Harvard Business Publishing:** Bellezza, S., Paharia, N. and Keinan, A. (2016). Conspicuous Consumption of Time: When Busyness and Lack of Leisure Time Become a Status Symbol. Journal of Consumer Research, Volume 44 (1), 118–138. Available from https://academic.oup.com/jcr/article/44/1/118/2736404 [Accessed 27 October 2019] 32 **William Penn:** Quoted by William Penn 33 **Tim Ferriss:** Quoted by Tim Ferriss 33 **Peter Drucker:** Quoted by Peter Drucker 51 **Andrew Carnegie:** Quoted by Andrew Carnegie 53 **Astro Teller:** Quoted by Astro Teller 62 **Mercer LLC:** 'Global Talent Trends 2019', Mercer 64 **Jacob Morgan:** Quoted by Jacob Morgan 67 **Deloitte:** What is the future of work?', Deloitte 68 **Catherine Bailey:** University of Sussex. (2017, June 14). 'Purposeful leaders' are winning hearts and minds in workplaces, study finds. ScienceDaily. Retrieved June 27, 2020 from www.sciencedaily.com/releases/2017/06/170614112908.htm 69 **Beth Ann Kaminkow:** Quoted by Beth Ann Kaminkow 69 **Kelly Choi:** Quoted by Kelly Choi

71 **Victor Frankl:** Quoted by Victor Frankl 73 **Simon Sinek:** Quoted by Simon Sinek 78 **Mabel Newcomer:** Quoted by Mabel Newcomer 78 **Ian Goodwin:** Quoted by Ian Goodwin 80 **Andrew Grove:** Quoted by Andrew Grove 85 **Chris Hadfield:** Quoted by Chris Hadfield 88 **KPMG:** KPMG, Benchmarking Innovation Impact 2020 89 **Eric Ries:** Quoted by Eric Ries 90 **Michael Schrage:** Quoted by Michael Schrage 90 **Laura Diamond:** Quoted by Laura Diamond 91 **Mark Zuckerberg:** Quoted by Mark Zuckerberg 91 **Caroline Webb:** Quoted by Caroline Webb 95 **Mabel Newcomer:** Quoted by Mabel Newcomer 95 **Walter Isaacson:** Quoted by Walter Isaacson 96 **Winston Churchill:** Quoted by Sir Winston Churchill 97 **Michael Schrage:** Quoted by Michael Schrage 102 **Babe Ruth:** Quoted by Babe Ruth 103 **Charles Duhigg:** Quoted by Charles Duhigg 104 **Anne Lewnes:** Quoted by Anne Lewnes 112 **Adam Henderson:** Quoted by Adam Henderson 119 **Daniel Coyle:** Quoted by Daniel Coyle 119 **Harvard Business Publishing:** Hill, L.A. et al. (2014). Collective Genius: The art and practice of leading innovation. Cambridge: Harvard Business Review Press 119 **Kim Scott:** Quoted by Kim Scott 129 **Reed Hastings:** Quoted by Reed Hastings 139 **John Doerr:** Quoted by John Doerr 139 **Grow:** Metric of the Week: North Star Metric. January 30, 2018 140 **Carl Hartman:** Quoted by Carl Hartman 141 **Antoine de Saint-Exupéry:** Quoted by Antoine de Saint-Exupéry 146 **Andrew Grove:** Quoted by Andrew Grove 147 **Marvin Bower:** Quoted by Marvin Bower 152 **Esther Perel:** Quoted by Esther Perel 153 **Michael Schrage:** Quoted by Michael Schrage 157 **Jennifer Whyte:** Quoted by Jennifer Whyte 157 **Klaus Schwab:** Quoted by Klaus Schwab 158 **Chris Hadfield:** Quoted by Chris Hadfield 160 **Harvard Business Publishing:** Van den Driest, F., Sthanunathan, S. and Weed, K. (2016). Building an Insights Engine. Harvard Business Review. Available from https://hbr.org/2016/09/building-an-insights-engine [Accessed 9 May 2020] 165 **Russ Wilson:** Quoted by Russ Wilson 172 **Manoush Zomorodi:** Quoted by Manoush Zomorodi 175 **John Gardner:** Quoted by John Gardner 177 **Michael Schrage:** Quoted by Michael Schrage 178 **Chris Sacca:** Quoted by Chris Sacca 178 **Teresa Amabile:** Quoted by Teresa Amabile 184 **Peter Drucker:** Quoted by Peter Drucker

186 David Foster Wallace: Quoted by David Foster Wallace **190 Michael Schrage:** Quoted by Michael Schrage **190 Patty McCord:** Quoted by Patty McCord **197 Steve Pitt:** Quoted by Steve Pitt **197 Daniel Coyle:** Quoted by Daniel Coyle **201 Bill Gates:** Quoted by Bill Gates **202 Klaus Schwab:** Quoted by Klaus Schwab **203 Greg Orme:** Quoted by Greg Orme **203 Henry Mason:** Quoted by Henry Mason **204 Henry Ford:** Quoted by Henry Ford **205 Michael Schrage:** Quoted by Michael Schrage **206 Pedro Uria-Reco:** Quoted by Pedro Uria-Reco **207 William Gibson:** Quoted by William Gibson **145 Ralph G. Nichols:** Quoted by Ralph G. Nichols

Foreword

Some years back, a clever and talented friend of mine was asked at a job interview whether he was a 'team player'. 'Yes,' he whimsically but cynically responded, 'Team captain'.

Pam Hamilton is not whimsically cynical. To the contrary, she's a cheerful pragmatist with a strong dash of idealism. But, like my friend, she prizes commitment to excellence over 'go along, get along' mediocrity. She sees talent, teams and teamwork being undervalued. That irks her. In real life and on these pages, she politely insists people offer the best of themselves and gives them the tools to do so. Pam would bring out the best in my whimsically cynical friend.

Even casual readers of *Supercharged Teams* will recognise it's written to be actively used, not passively read. Something is wrong if you don't feel compelled to test and explore its advice. That's her intent. Pam's focus on making her real-world facilitative and workshop experiences accessible, as well as actionable, is impressive. Her respect and concern for her readers reflect the respect and concern she has for her clients.

I cannot overemphasise this point: this book is about real people on real teams in the real world, not idealised frameworks contingent upon the 'right' people at the 'right' time all getting together to do the 'right' thing. Supercharged teams avoid the soul-sucking drain of nicks, cuts and compromises done for comity's sake. Empowering healthy high performance is what leadership needs to mean. Pam describes principles and practices that simultaneously challenge people while making it easier for them to take the next step. That duality makes Pam's methodology distinctive and valuable.

That value becomes even clearer during pandemic times. Enforced remoteness, digital technologies and networked collaboration have pushed people to revisit and rethink team dynamics. The fundamentals are more important than ever. How can remote teams creatively incorporate client perspectives? What makes diversity and inclusion a source of energy and inspiration? What makes 'leading by example' not just possible but inevitable? What makes your team so special?

Leaderships worldwide struggle for good – even great – answers while coping with remarkably unfair and burdensome constraints. Yet that is precisely why we need 'supercharged' teams – because yesterday's answers aren't capable of rising to the occasion. Talented teams need guidance, they need structure, they need tools and they need self-awareness. These are what *Supercharged Teams* provides.

The surest sign this book 'works' will not be your delight, enlightenment or agreement (although those are important). The key metric will be what you share with your colleagues and teammates. They are your partners, they are your complements, they are your support. What will you share with them that can better bring out their best?

The great thing about *Supercharged Teams* is that this question is not rhetorical; it's why Pam crafted this book. It's why you should read it and use it.

Michael Schrage
May 2020

What this book will give you

Working in a team is harder than ever – work is faster, leaner and busier – and we forget that teamwork needs work. *Supercharged Teams: 30 Tools of Great Teamwork* gives you the tools you need to get the best from your team. Featuring the latest approaches used by high-performing teams around the world, this book will supercharge you and your team to perform and succeed.

Work is changing, and the rules of being in a team have changed. We are time-poor, attention-starved, pressured to work faster and better, more often working remotely and in different locations. It's easy to feel overloaded, and doing great teamwork can be the last thing on our list of priorities.

The work teams have to do is also changing. New technologies and market disruption create complex challenges that can only be solved by experts working well together, whether they are in the same office or have to work across different departments and organisations. Not only is working better together the right thing to do but it's the only way we will succeed on the complex issues we face today.

The good news is that everything that stands in the way of good teamwork can be overcome with the right tools. This book gives you the power to make sure your team succeeds in today's challenging working environments. You will find:

- Thirty tools to supercharge you, your team and the way your team works.
- Techniques to rethink, challenge and evaluate your team at every level, whether you lead a team or belong to one.
- A clear understanding of how work is changing, and the best approaches to be an effective team in today's work environment.
- Case studies and real-world examples from companies like Unilever, Diageo, Essity, AB InBev, Netflix, BAE Systems, Ipsos, WPP and public-sector examples from local councils, charities and the voluntary and community sector to bring the tools to life.
- The power to supercharge your team, today.

chapter 1

Why supercharge your team?

Alone we can do so little; together we can do so much.

Helen Keller (1880–1968)

Once there was a group of people who had a unique opportunity to change how the world worked together, for the better. That time is now, and we are those people. We are living in a time of unprecedented change, when all teams have to perform at the very edge of their capabilities. Teams and teamwork are being tested and challenged at every level. Today 'good enough' is no longer enough. We have a rare chance to use this period of disruption and innovation to evolve how we work. For every single team in the world, now is the time to supercharge. If not now, when?

Over the last two decades, I've worked with thousands of teams around the world, from small local charities to huge global corporations. I've experienced a range of team dynamics, from the truly excellent to the very dysfunctional. As a team member I've been inspired by the clever, creative people I've worked with, and I've been disillusioned by the bullies and bad behaviour that inevitably emerge in any human situation.

As a lifetime psychology student and a committed people watcher, I have always been fascinated by how people behave in groups. In my work as a consultant, I am invited into teams as an independent facilitator, and can observe with an outsider's perspective. I've seen similar patterns of behaviours across all the teams I've met, no matter what the culture, company or size, and if you have ever worked in a team, I suspect we share similar experiences.

Supercharged teams operate on a different level, way above average. They are driven by the energy of a powerful vision, an urgent sense of purpose, and the motivation to work well together because they know that is the only way they will achieve, even exceed, their goals. Today, every team in the world has to solve complex problems and create new opportunities to do their best work, whether for clients, customers, consumers or each other. The difference between going through the motions and truly performing with momentum is making a deliberate choice to supercharge.

Teams solve more problems and create more opportunities than any one person could achieve alone. High-performing teams can overcome challenges and achieve real impact together. Being part of a brilliant team can be an overwhelmingly positive experience and great teams don't only feel good, they also achieve more. On the complex issues we need to solve, like the environment, social inequality, economic disruption, immigration and refugees, we need true collaboration and incredible teamwork more than ever.

However, good teamwork doesn't come naturally. Because of different priorities and personality types, people don't automatically manage to work well together. True collaboration is always difficult because we all carry our own working styles, preconceptions and expectations into any team. Poor-performing teams aren't just inefficient, they stifle the intelligence and purpose of the people in them, leaving them less capable and unmotivated.

Teams are like families. We share a common experience and build relationships, habits and behaviours together over time, but even if we love and trust each other, we don't give the same amount of respect or effort to each other that we would to strangers. In pressured situations, or when things change, we fall back on old ways of doing things, some of which may not be effective in the new situation. The better a team knows each other and the longer they have worked together, the worse the potential for dysfunction is.

I believe we assign people to teams far too readily and we need to work in fewer teams for more effective work. I need to confess that I sometimes wish I didn't have to work in teams. It is sometimes easier to avoid all the difficulty of collaborating. However, there's no escaping it, and the research proves time and again that teams achieve more than individuals working alone, particularly in today's rapidly evolving world. The problem is that the way we work today has changed, but the way we work in teams has not, and it needs to.

Great things in business are never done by one person; they're done by a team of people.

Steve Jobs (1955–2011)

Why do we need supercharged teams?

Being in a team used to be a lot simpler. Team meetings were an efficient use of time because they allowed for quality thinking and considered decision-making. A regular meeting helped teams to stay aligned and protected our time outside of the meeting for actions. Between meetings, we had one-to-one conversations and shared this information with the whole team when we got together. It's no surprise that work felt less pressured, as our working patterns were more predictable, communication was at a manageable pace, information was limited, and the time between working and meetings was distinct.

How the world has changed. Markets are being disrupted by technology and innovation, and the way we serve our consumers, customers and clients has shifted remarkably. What we are working on has changed – we have more information for decision-making than ever before. Our work is more complex, across different platforms and via new channels. It is almost impossible to be an expert on everything, so knowledge needs to be shared between different specialists.

How we work has also changed. Technology has helped us to collaborate faster, but it has also reduced our attention, time and focus on our work. We are less likely to work face to face, and remote and flexible working are already both commonplace and causing huge challenges to the way we work in teams.

Definitions

- **Remote working:** People working from different locations, not in the same office.
- **Flexible working:** People working specific hours, times of day, days of the week or months of the year, not 9 am–5 pm.
- **Gig-style jobs:** People contracted temporarily to complete a specific task, either as a contractor or as an employee.

Around the world, even before COVID-19, 70% of full-time professionals worked remotely at least one day a week. In the UK, the gig economy has more than doubled in the last three years and now accounts for more than 4.7 million workers.[1] Between 2008 and 2016 the number of freelancers in the UK increased by 36%,[2] and in the coming years, 79% of executives expect that contingent and freelance workers will substantially replace full-time employees.[3] A 2019 study commissioned by Timewise found that the number of highly paid jobs offered part-time or with flexible hours has trebled in the past four years, as workers turn their back on the nine-to-five.[4]

Against this background of change, isn't it crazy that we are all trying to work in the same way that we always did, only faster? We continue to create and join teams blindly, using inherited team cultures and processes, without considering how teams need to work to perform well today. We don't invest in teamwork or nurture our teams, and we are less likely to see examples of great teamwork to inspire us. We are at risk today of doing worse teamwork than ever before.

> **Research consistently shows that teams underperform, despite all the extra resources they have.**
>
> **J Richard Hackman[5]**

It is no longer enough to join a team and assume it will achieve something. Whether you belong to a team or lead one, you can be the catalyst that resets your team to high performance, with the right tools.

What is a team?

A team is a group of people who work together to achieve a common goal, and it consists of more than one person. Teamwork is the ability of a group of people to work together effectively to achieve that goal. Team members:

- each have relevant expertise
- work effectively together
- achieve more than they would working separately
- work towards an agreed goal

- have a defined deadline
- are accountable for the decisions they make
- have the influence to deliver the team objective

Over the last decade, scientists at MIT have worked to understand and measure 'collective intelligence'.[6] Similar to an IQ test, it determines how well groups solve problems together. Their research has proved time and again that teams can create more successful results than the most intelligent person in that team could create alone.

Businesses have recognised this – the amount of teamwork we do is definitely increasing. The *Harvard Business Review* found that in the last two decades, time spent in collaboration activities has increased by 50%.[7] This is because collaboration is the only way to solve the complex business problems we now face, but it has also led to 'collaborative overload'. We are called on to join more and more teams and our time and attention, and therefore our effectiveness, are diluted.

How do supercharged teams do it?

When we join a team it's tempting to focus on how often we'll meet and what the meeting agenda will be, without considering who is on the team with us: are they the right people; do they have the time; will this work be motivating to them? We also need to consider whether we have the right ambition in mind and how we will make sure to work together well. We cannot ignore who our stakeholders are, how our leaders can support us, and how the culture we work in will affect our team. Successful teams consider all of these.

According to MIT,[8] a successful team has the following factors:

- A shared understanding of the team's mission
- A commitment to the team's goals
- Clearly defined roles and responsibilities
- Agreed-upon ground rules

- An established decision-making model
- Effective ways of working together

You may have heard of approaches to teamwork like Agile Teams or Scrums – these are the kinds of teams that work well today. No matter the name, what these have in common is a shared purpose based on a clear, defined task, with a diverse group of experts who come together efficiently to achieve something in a set timeframe, working with momentum to overcome the challenges they face because they have set themselves up to do so.

Types of high-performing team

Type of team	How they work	Examples
Agile teams	A small group of people, assigned to the same project, nearly all of them working on a full-time basis to deliver value to users, customers, services or stakeholders against a specific objective.	A group of people taken out of their day jobs for two months to work together on how to make products and services more sustainable across the business, with a presentation to the board at the end of the project to bid for money to fund specific ideas.
Scrums or Sprint teams	People working together to deliver requested and committed product increments, often at a very fast pace or over a short duration. Everyone within the team follows a common goal, agrees to the rules of the team and respects each other to ensure they work together in the most productive way towards a solution.	A hackathon event that brings together software developers, designers, engineers and clients to collaborate intensively to solve a particular software problem over one weekend.

Type of team	How they work	Examples
Project teams or cross-functional teams	A group of people from different departments or with diverse expertise who work together to deliver an objective within a limited time period, collaborating to use the best of their diverse expertise.	A cross-company team set up to deliver a new ice-cream innovation product launch before the summer season.
Action groups or task forces	A group who have come together to respond to a threat, situation or issue that requires urgent action via investigation, decision-making and implementation of ideas by a specific date.	A local government group including health, housing, police, faith groups and charities to work together to reduce the number of rough sleepers by Christmas.

No matter how brilliant your mind or strategy, if you're playing a solo game, you'll always lose out to a team.

Reid Hoffman[9]

So, what is the difference between being a good enough team versus a high-performing one? High-performing teams *deliberately and consciously* agree on the right mindset, pace and approach they will use to work well together, based on the task at hand. They don't have the same team, or ways of working, or timing or regular meetings on every project, they reset them for each specific project.

When you are training to be a pilot, you learn about the Eastern Air Lines Flight 401, an aviation accident that happened in 1972. The crew had become so fixated on a burnt-out landing gear light that they didn't notice that the autopilot had become disengaged and the flight was descending, ultimately crashing into the Florida Everglades.[10] Learning from this accident led to the creation of CRM, standard procedures used by the aviation industry worldwide ever since to help crews work better together, effectively and safely, in any situation they find themselves in.[11]

In 2008, the World Health Organisation found that more than 60% of patients worldwide had key safety measures missed during surgery.[12] Atul Gawande, a doctor and surgeon, helped to create a simple one-page surgical checklist for surgery teams to go through to improve the way surgery teams worked together, which resulted in substantial reductions in complications and deaths and is now used worldwide.[13]

In both aviation and medicine, technology continues to advance, but the difference between failure and success is whether the people using it work well together as a team. Successful teams use simple tools like CRM and the surgical checklist to give them a structure that helps them collaborate better. Whether you are a member of a team, or its leader, the best way you can make sure a team achieves its goals is to consciously check in with your team, resetting it for effective delivery, using a clear framework of tools. This book gives you the tools you need to supercharge your team.

How to use the 30 tools of great teamwork

The 30 tools of great teamwork are organised across 12 chapters. Some tools will work better than others depending on your specific challenges, so choose those that make the most sense to your team. All of the tools can be used by any team, whether they work in the same building or remotely in different time zones.

You may choose to work through each tool in order as you begin a new team or reset an existing one, or you may choose to go straight to the chapter or tool that your team would most benefit from. Each tool will work as a stand-alone exercise, and they can be used in any order.

Each chapter begins with a 'What you will learn in this chapter' summary, and has 'Key take outs' at the end. In the final chapter there are some workshop outlines that will help you apply the relevant tools to your team. Here is an overview of the chapters and tools for you to choose from:

Chapter 2: Choose your team

We need strong teams more than ever before, and today's working environment cries out for better teamwork. However, being in a team can be a default assumption instead of a conscious decision. Some tasks are great for teams to work on, but others are better done by individuals. Use these tools to assess the task, decide if a team is required, and choose the right team.

> **Tool 1:** To team or not to team – do you really need a team?
>
> **Tool 2:** Turning a group into a team – make a group of people into a team
>
> **Tool 3:** Choose, avoid or separate – choose the right team members for your team

Chapter 3: Find more time

Being too busy is common at work, but having the time to participate properly in a team is key. Prioritising what your team spends time on is crucial to success. These tools will create more time and impact for your team.

> **Tool 4:** The timetable – measure where you spend your time and stop wasting it
>
> **Tool 5:** Meeting sharpeners – make meetings shorter and sharper
>
> **Tool 6:** Email agreement – set email etiquette to reduce time on email

Chapter 4: What goals do you want to achieve?

Success means different things to different people. A crucial stage in setting team ambition is to define what a successful outcome is early on. These tools will help to create a powerful vision of what success looks like, reframe and clarify project outcomes, and align your team with a clear direction from the start.

Tool 7: Five futures – define a successful vision of your project

Tool 8: Reframe your aim – make your team's objective more inspiring and ambitious

Tool 9: Project navigator – align your team on a project scope from the beginning

Chapter 5: Find your motivation

Working in a team can be hard and tiring, and sometimes it's hard to find the motivation to keep going. However, if the work gives us a sense of purpose and helps us achieve a personal ambition beyond the project, it makes us motivated to achieve more together. Use these tools to enhance the meaning of your work for you and for the team.

Tool 10: Define team purpose – why are you doing what you're doing?

Tool 11: Why our work matters – create awareness of the positive impact of your work

Tool 12: Personal motivators – how can you benefit from your team's work?

Chapter 6: Agree what you will deliver, and when

Agreeing on what the team will deliver, by when, is a first step in any team. Rather than making assumptions or accepting a directive without question, these tools help you to interrogate your task, project and journey early to make the best use of your team's time.

Tool 13: The journey plan – create a roadmap to your goal that includes the challenges you may face and milestones to track your progress

Tool 14: Accelerate and reflect – create a timeline that prioritises actions and includes time for reflection and refinement

Tool 15: Measuring success checklist – plan to measure the success of your project outcomes, outputs and journey

Chapter 7: Ways to work together

The way a team works together should be conscious and agreed, not based on habit. When a team commits to specific behaviours and ways of working, they can hold each other to account and get the most from each other. Use these tools to agree how to work together and safely reset any ineffective team behaviours.

Tool 16: Three-point check-in – build trust and develop empathy between team members

Tool 17: Our team rules – deliberately choose the team's rules of engagement

Tool 18: Distance culture code – set up the best ways of working if your team is in different locations

Chapter 8: Dealing with conflict

Relationships between team members can be difficult, and teams will inevitably face conflict. These tools help you to set roles and expectations to avoid conflict, manage it when it does arise, restore harmony, and deal with difficult behaviours in your team.

Tool 19: Opinions and instincts – identify disagreement and misalignment early on

Tool 20: Conflict predictor – predict the conflicts that might arise and avoid them

Tool 21: Six reasons why – learn from recent issues and prevent them from reoccurring

Tool 22: Individual intervention – address conflict with an individual in your team

Chapter 9: Get support from leaders

The environment the team works in makes a big difference to how effective the team is. If the team is not sponsored by decision-makers and key influencers, or does not support the organisation's direction of travel, the efforts of the team can be wasted. These tools help you get the support you need from the leaders who can support your teamwork.

Tool 23: Direction of travel – understand your leaders' targets so you know if you're going in the right direction

Tool 24: Leader listening tool – really listen to your leader to develop true connection and understanding between you

Tool 25: Customer quiz – connect leaders with their customers

Chapter 10: Engage your stakeholders

Every team works on behalf of a wider group, and keeping those stakeholders updated can be difficult. If you give them too much information, you can get thrown off track if they interfere, but if you keep information back, you risk not getting support or approval at later stages. Use these tools to give your stakeholders regular, useful and constructive updates that don't hold your teamwork back.

Tool 26: Secret stakeholder survey – understand what your stakeholders think

Tool 27: Building session – get your stakeholders to build on the team's work

Tool 28: Start well, end well – start and end stakeholder meetings constructively

Chapter 11: Build a new culture

Any successful team needs to understand the culture they are working in. Whether understanding customers in a new way, or adopting new ideas, or working differently, teams often need to help people to change what they do. These tools give you some simple ways to help your project outcomes succeed rather than be rejected.

Tool 29: Code your culture – understand what shapes the culture, and why this is the case

Tool 30: Create your culture – begin culture change with your team

Chapter 12: What do teams look like in the future?

Our working worlds will continue to change and the technology, social, employment and economic trends of today will continue to grow. Successful teams will learn and adapt ever more frequently to stay effective. The ability to supercharge our teams is crucial to our teamwork now and will be even more important in future.

Chapter 13: Using *Supercharged Teams* and 30 tools in your team

Use the 30 tools of great teamwork to reset your team, with three different workshop approaches. Whether you are working in a small or large team, face to face, in the same building or across the world from each other, this set of tools will help you as a team member or leader to reset your ways of working and achieve your goals.

We now have the responsibility and the permission to supercharge our teams, and we can do this by deliberately resetting how our team works together, using these tools.

chapter 2

Choose your team

A supercharged team starts with having the best people on the team. But before we choose them, do we need a team? Some tasks can only be done by a team, but others are better done alone. If you already belong to a team, ask yourself if it is truly a team, or are you a group of people working in parallel with each other but without clear goals? Whether you are in a team or choosing one, you can supercharge it.

The driving force behind this chapter is to eradicate the 'committee', an incumbent group of people who spend all their energy organising meetings, agreeing agendas and writing, distributing and reviewing minutes, and far too little time on the ideas, actions and impact of their work, or indeed doing anything beyond attending meetings.

If we want a supercharged team, we need to be clear that the task needs a team, that we have chosen the right, tight team of people who will create real impact against clear goals.

What you will learn in this chapter:

- How to decide if a team is the right approach.
- How to know if you're a team, or something that calls itself a team but isn't.

- How to turn a group of people into a team.
- How to put a team together . . .
- . . . and how to manage people you wouldn't choose but are required to have on your team.

Do you need a team?

We tend to assume that every problem can be solved by a team. We start and join multiple teams and committees in the hope they will achieve something, but we don't always consider whether this is the right way to achieve the goal, or whether the people on the team have the time and expertise to properly contribute. When we blindly assign people to teams or invite them to regular update meetings, we hope they will naturally achieve something together. But not all teams do. Without the right people, direction and leadership, teams can be a waste of time.

Even when you are working on a great project, teamwork can be slower and more frustrating than working alone. You might spend your time debating with other people instead of getting on with it, and this could slow you down and dilute your impact. If your work can be done by one person, don't start a team. If we want to supercharge our work, we should only create or join a team when we know it's the best way to achieve true impact, not as a default solution to every goal.

Tool 1

To team or not to team

Use this tool to identify whether you need a team at all, or if you can do the work without one. Don't waste time in a team if the work can be done by one person. Instead leave people the time to join teams that need them.

Can be done alone	Needs a team
I know what needs to be done and I can do it myself	I'm not sure what the right direction is and need other people to inform my decisions
I am the main decision-maker, and as long as I have a strong argument people will support what I decide	I will need information and ideas from other people, and show I have included them in this decision
I have enough time to get this done alone	I need more people to help me do this before the deadline
The issue is straightforward, but it needs a bit of thinking through by someone	The issue is complicated and needs different experts to work it all out
My colleagues and my boss will challenge and add to my thinking when I present my ideas to them	My colleagues and boss can't provide all the advice or expertise required so I need to bring in other experts to get the best thinking and ideas
This needs project management, someone to check that everyone has done what they were supposed to do by each deadline	This is more than project management – we need to discuss and debate ideas at each stage, and decide how to move forward together

A committee is a cul-de-sac down which ideas are lured and then quietly strangled.

Sir Barnett Cocks, 1907–1989

Are we a team or not?

You are a team only if you work together towards an agreed goal with specific objectives and deadlines. A group of people who work in the same office or meet regularly are not automatically a team.

A department is not a team. You may find that the reason you are not performing well as a team is that you are not really a team at all – you are a group of people working together but without a direction or deliverable. If you are a committee, work group or simply meet regularly to share information, it will be hard to achieve anything without shared goals or deadlines, especially if you are not delivering something that has a measurable, positive impact outside your meetings.

Essity

Teamwork is wanting to win together

Gael De Talhouet, Essity's Vice President, Brand Building, describes the company as 'people-focused'. Respect and care are anchored in its Swedish culture and courage is one of the company's beliefs and behaviours, enabling people to speak freely and sometimes 'confront the uncomfortable'. Taking teamwork for granted is one such uncomfortable misunderstanding that Gael suggests we need to confront, saying 'putting half a dozen people in a room and asking them to work on a common objective does not create a team'. Distinguishing collaboration from teamwork is critical, he says. While collaboration can force people with different personal values and different objectives for a project (or a personal agenda) to work together, teams share common values, a common team spirit, and build on each other's energy.

Teamwork is wanting to win together and creates a much higher level of energy than collaboration, and that spark of energy makes the team achieve the unexpected. The added value of a leader is to turn collaboration into teamwork.

Tool 2

Turning a group into a team

You can only supercharge if you have a true team. Use this table to identify whether you are working in a group rather than a team, and if you are, what you need to do to become a team.

Type of group	Group definition	The group becomes a team if
Work group, working group or standing group	A group of people who sit in the same office or work in the same company for broad company goals, but don't deliver any specific projects together	A selection of people from this group are chosen for their expertise and are responsible for delivering specific, measurable actions, changes or ideas for the company against a deadline
Committee	A group of people who meet regularly to update each other and share information, and check on roles, responsibilities and actions done between meetings	The committee agrees an event, initiative or change to make, with an agreed goal and deadline to achieve it by, and work as a collaborative team beyond committee meeting times to do so
A team meeting or update meeting	A group of people who meet regularly to update each other on their separate work, but take away no actions from the meeting and don't work together between meetings	The group agrees a direction, strategy or initiative they want to achieve together, and takes on actions between updates, working together to achieve their goal

Type of group	Group definition	The group becomes a team if
Think tank	A group of people who work together to analyse information and create thinking, white papers or best practice to inform decisions taken by other groups	The group creates ideas on how to action or implement the thinking in a live environment, beyond the theoretical, and takes part in the action to make this happen
Workshop or brainstorm	A group of people who get together for an away day or time out of their day jobs to create new ideas	A group agrees actions from the workshop, and aligns on the ideas to take forward, sharing actions to make these happen
Inspiration or information-sharing group	A group of people who choose to share inspiration and information with each other to enrich their work and share best practice	The group uses the inspiration or information to inform an action plan or project inspired by the information, and takes actions between meetings to implement these
Company board or board meeting	A group of board members who meet to discuss company progress, strategic developments and compliance	The board agrees a specific project or strategy to achieve by a deadline, and defines the milestones and actions that will enable this to happen, with each board member taking actions to complete between meetings

Choosing the right team

It may seem silly to say this, but if you're going to lead a team, you ought to first make sure that you know who's on it.

J Richard Hackman[1]

Not only must we consciously choose to be a team, we must choose the right people too. It often feels easier to work with the same people you've worked with before, but high-performing teams deliberately choose the best team members to work with.

There are three principles to consider when you are choosing the right team:[2]

1 Diverse backgrounds
2 Mix of personality types
3 Fewer team members

Diverse backgrounds

Creating a diverse team is absolutely crucial to success, not only for avoiding groupthink but for creating successful impact. And yet it is hard to create diverse teams – most people want to hire themselves. Ethnic diversity is important, as is diversity of backgrounds, past roles, age, expertise and life experience.

'Groupthink' or 'herd mentality' is what happens when a team of people are more focussed on agreeing with each other than on the quality of their decisions.[3] Diversity in all forms prevents this.

Plenty of research has found that diversity makes teams more successful. One study proved that mixed ethnicity teams were more accurate on pricing and had fewer trading errors in live financial markets, whether they were based in South-east Asia or North America. Ethnically diverse teams were 58% more accurate, and the researchers believe this is because when you are all from the same background, you are more likely to agree with each other, whereas mixed groups are more likely to challenge or question each other's thinking, and this 'creates friction that helps decision-making because it stops conformity'.[4]

BAE Systems

Diverse teams

As Products and Training Services Director at BAE Systems, the defence, aerospace and security company, Brooke Hoskins leads a team of 1,200 people. Brooke deliberately encourages diversity in the teams she leads, whether in terms of gender, ethnicity, background, or experience and even personality type. She told me different perspectives have a very positive impact on the way people work together, the number of ideas, how they get delivered and the energy in the room.

In her experience a team who are all alike might find it easier to get along, but don't necessarily produce the best work. When diverse teams work together it may take longer and be more challenging because they don't always agree at first, and so take longer to get there, but when they do, Brooke finds the results are far better.

Mix of personality types

There is no doubt that people influence each other's moods, motivation and energy levels. While it's unreasonable to expect that people will be on their best behaviour every time they meet, do consider the mix of personality types and working styles in your team, as they will make a difference to how the team works together and on the successful delivery of your work.

First, make sure your team is made up of 'problem owners' not 'problem moaners'. Problem owners feel invested in understanding the problem and share responsibility for solving it with the rest of the team. They create energy by being challenging, opinionated and passionate, and hold other team members to account if they are at risk of making the wrong decision. Problem owners want to solve the problem and find the answer. Problem moaners, however, focus on the problems and either do not want to solve them or believe they cannot be solved. They are so focused on what is wrong with every idea that they cannot offer alternatives, and they have a severely negative influence on the rest of the team.

When selecting a team, leaders need to ask themselves: 'Who inspires me and helps me to learn new things?' They also need to ask: 'Who are the vampires who suck the group's time and energy without giving anything back? So, when I build teams to take on complex challenges, I look to surround myself with people who fuel, rather than extinguish, the group's enthusiasm for exploration.'

Greg Orme[5]

This is not to say you should only have optimists on your team. Having constructive cynics on the team is essential. Constructive cynics have a lot of experience, represent the sceptical views of other stakeholders, and challenge the team's assumptions. They point out potential errors early and help the team to avoid the obvious, lowest common denominator conclusions that groupthink can create. The constructive cynic wants the project to succeed and is throwing up the challenges that need to be overcome for success.

If there's one thing that makes me cynical, it's optimists.

Julian Baggini[6]

ITV

Optimism can be destructive

I am an optimist by nature, but over the years I've realised that unbridled optimism can be just as destructive as complete cynicism. In 2006 I was recruited as Head of Creative Development at ITV Imagine, a central innovation team responsible for innovating content at ITV. I had come from the world of innovation for consumer goods companies like Unilever and Kraft foods, where we had to really work hard to encourage corporate teams to be more creative.

In the first couple of creative workshops I led, I hadn't realised how patronising it was to tell TV people how to be more creative, and nor had I fully understood the extent to which in a creative culture ideas are closely guarded. My optimism did not triumph, and those first workshops were not a success to put it mildly. I distinctly remember one person going back to their manager and saying 'Please never make me do that again.' I was naive and had completely underestimated the creative talent I was working with. These were people who'd spent their lives being creative without me telling them how. We learned our lessons and very successfully worked for many years afterwards with TV creatives by instead curating experiences designed to inspire them, rather than teaching them the principles of creativity.

Be careful when choosing optimists in your team. They are great for new ideas and positive thinking, but if the ideas are random, naive or irrelevant, they can be as exhausting as a destructive cynic on the energy levels of the team.

Fewer team members

Research into the ideal team suggests that ten people or fewer make the best team.[7] Ten people can work effectively and efficiently, develop strong relationships, and won't get bogged down by too many people being involved in scheduling, information-sharing and decision-making. Smaller teams have less conflict, more cohesion,[8] and achieve better outcomes.[9]

The problem is people don't want to be left out, particularly of exciting or high-profile projects, and before you know it everyone and anyone who may have an interest is part of the team, and most of the time is spent trying to coordinate when the team can meet instead of what the team can do.

For your supercharged team, don't have more than ten members, or if you have to, see whether you can split into sub-teams on specific goals, and meet with the rest of the team at regular intervals when needed.

Tool 3

Choose, avoid or separate

Being an effective team means saying no to some people joining your team. Use this checklist to make sure you are choosing the right mix of people for your team and avoiding the wrong people, so you can keep the highest performers. If there are people who need to be involved, separate them so they don't drag your team down.

Choose people who	Avoid people who
Are experts or have lots of experience	Are so senior they scare people
Bring fresh thinking and will challenge the team	Are cynical, bored or bitter about the project
Are energetic, curious, positive and enthusiastic	Are very junior, inexperienced or over-simplify the issues

Choose people who	Avoid people who
Want to be on the team to learn new skills	Believe they already know the answer and won't change their minds
Are different in profile to the rest of the team	Bring no diversity of experience or background to the team
Have the deep technical knowledge that this project needs	Are there because they don't want to be left out
Have the time to commit to meetings and actions	Want to be there but don't have time to attend fully or do any actions
Will collaborate well and treat team members with respect	Don't believe in collaboration, bully or dominate other people

Or separate

We often group the most difficult, senior or challenging team members together, separating them from the core team so they can get on with their work. Treat them as stakeholders and give them regular updates, gathering their ideas to share with the team, but keep them separate from the team so they don't hold the team back. Selecting people for how well they work together is just as important as bringing in the right expertise. Protecting the whole team from one individual's working style may be necessary to help the team succeed. Otherwise, it will keep your team from being supercharged.

See more on how to deal with difficult personalities in Chapter 8 'Dealing with conflict', and engaging senior people in Chapter 10 'Engage your stakeholders'.

Deliberately select your supercharged team

Attending meetings is not the same as being in a team. If you want a supercharged team, don't blindly create or join one. Instead, think about the goal and who will give your team the best chance to succeed. Fight against the temptation to inherit old teams. In an effective, high-performing team, every team member is there for a reason, so choose to be a team, and choose who is in your team deliberately.

Key take outs

- -

- Not everything needs to be done by a team – sometimes the best way to get something done is to do it yourself.
- A team is a team only if it has a shared goal that everybody works together to achieve.
- A group of people can become a team if they commit to a common goal and work collaboratively to achieve it.
- An effective team is small, diverse and includes particular personality types.
- Non-collaborators can be worked with outside of the team to contribute to achieving the team's goal.

chapter 3

Find more time

Supercharged teams prioritise their time to maximise impact. Having the time to be in a team is crucial to success. If your team doesn't have time to fully participate, the team will not achieve its goals. One day we will look back on the way we work now with disbelief and ask ourselves how we found ourselves working on so much, at such a pace, with such poor attention and quality thinking. We are all far too busy, and one of the biggest challenges we face is finding the time to work well as a team. 'Fire-fighting' or doing short-term, urgent work on unexpected problems becomes common when people are under pressure. When our time is taken up by urgent work, we don't have time to build relationships with each other, and we don't work on our team's longer-term objectives.

In my first job I was Marketing Assistant at Wallace Laboratories in Zimbabwe. I had a desk phone, a paper diary and a pad of paper, and no mobile, computer, printer or screens. We would phone people up and talk, or we would meet in person. We discussed decisions and actions. We sent memos beforehand or minutes afterwards, but most of our time was spent in conversation, understanding each other. Now, we barely have the time to talk with our colleagues, much less discuss important decisions or create new ideas.

Carving out time and prioritising where you spend your energy is the only way you will become a supercharged team. Taking control of our own time is critical to success, and if we don't manage, we will never succeed. Work will keep getting busier and the answer is not to put our heads down and work harder.

The tools in this chapter will give you and your team the gift of time. By helping you identify the black holes where your time is wasted, understanding where most impact can be made, and making sure your time is valued and used well, we can help you move from fire-fighting to making progress.

What you will learn in this chapter:

- How the team can identify and reduce time-wasting activities to spend more time on more effective and impactful work.

- How to stop other people from using up your precious time so that you can more fully participate in your team and do more quality work.

- How to reduce time spent unnecessarily on emails to make space for relationship building and quality thinking.

- How to sharpen up your team meetings so that you can use your team's time more efficiently and get more done.

You need time to be in a team

It's really clear that the most precious resource we all have is time.

Steve Jobs (1955–2011)

When someone asks us to join a team, it's tempting to agree without considering if we have the time. Perhaps we don't think we can say no, or we are not given a choice, and when we join teams like this we try to do as little as possible. However, for a team to do really good work together, every member needs to have the time to be present and to actively contribute to the team's goals. Simply turning up at meetings does not make you part of a team.

We can't create more hours in the day, but we can and must create more time by becoming more efficient and selective about where we expend our effort. We need to have the time to participate in a team if we want that team to be supercharged, and we need to create this time by taking it away from somewhere else. In her book *Fully Connected*, Julia Hobsbawm talks about how important it is for people and organisations to manage their time in a balanced way so that they can flourish and be productive without being overwhelmed.[1] We can only flourish and be productive, and have the ability to manage all our knowledge and networks if we manage our own time.

Being busy is no longer a status symbol

A busy and overworked lifestyle, rather than a leisurely lifestyle, has become an aspirational status symbol . . . people dread idleness and desire busyness in search of meaning and motivation in their lives.

Silvia Bellezza[2]

When people ask you how you are, do you say, 'I'm busy' instead of 'I'm fine'? Being too busy is all too common, and for some people it is the way they show they are doing well, in demand, working hard, and are important. But why is being busy considered impressive, aspirational or positive? Being too busy means we have been unable to plan our own time, we are at the mercy of other people's expectations, or we are not being selective about where to focus our attention and energy. This is not something to be proud of. It might be something to share because we are struggling and need help, but being too busy is no longer something to boast about.

Let's agree that busyness, full calendars, long to-do lists and lack of time are not status symbols, and instead focus on the core and substance of the work we produce. Being busy means nothing if we are not achieving something with our work.

Work will keep getting busier

Time is what we want most, but what we use worst.

William Penn (1644–1718)

We all feel greater time pressure than ever before. Companies are increasing their drive for efficiency, smaller teams are doing the work that larger teams used to do, roles have changed and combined to create multiple objectives, and we are given ever more challenging tasks. So, the work we are doing feels and is much more complicated than it ever was. No wonder we feel too busy.

The way we communicate is also making us busier. Sending messages and sharing information digitally rather than speaking feels easier and more instant, whether you are working across different time zones, different locations, or even when you are in the same room. This back and forth style means that we are under pressure to reply quickly, rather than considering a quality answer or suggestion. This means we make more mistakes, whether we don't think before we reply, or we use a tone that may sound negative because we are in a rush.

There's no doubt there is more to do than ever before, but the same amount of time to do it in. It is tempting to think that 'work harder, do more' is the answer, and indeed that is how most people try to keep up; checking messages during meetings, emailing while they travel, using any downtime for catching up. It's a trap we all fall into – we think that if we can just get on top of things, it will get better. But we are deluding ourselves because there will only be more to do, not less.

Saying' keep up', 'put your head down', or 'work harder' is not useful. The pace will keep getting faster as we have access to more and more information. Just trying harder can lead to burnout, mistakes and stress, which are destructive for teams and their work.

Email is not our main job

A 2018 study of 2,000 US knowledge workers showed that poorly used meetings and email topped the list of things that keep workers from getting work done. The same report showed that after emails, meetings, interruptions and admin, the average worker has just 44% of their time left to do their job.[3]

I don't know anyone whose job is to 'do' email. It is a useful tool, but we treat it like it's our main work. Email is a sort of professional candy crush, something that we do when we want to be doing something useful, but don't have the energy to work on something important. We are addicted to it, but it wastes our time.

More email does not mean better teamwork! Sending more emails gives us more to do, read and respond to, which makes us less productive because we don't have time to connect with each other properly, or do quality thinking, because we are too busy on emails. It's distracting and gets in the way of quality thinking and building relationships with our team members.

Being busy is a form of laziness – lazy thinking and indiscriminate action. Being busy is most often used as a guise for avoiding the few critically important but uncomfortable actions.

Tim Ferriss[4]

Tool 4

The timetable

You can't manage what you can't measure.

Peter Drucker (1909–2005)

If you are struggling to find enough quality time for your team, you need to find more time, and to do that you need to measure where your time is being spent. If you take the time to do the timetable, it is guaranteed to save you time!

1 Record the number of hours you spend in a normal working week on different tasks and meetings.

---

2 Put them in order of time, starting with the tasks that take the most time at the top.

3 Colour-code the impact and importance of each task based on how much they help you achieve your main objectives at work (green: directly helps me achieve my work objectives; orange: important to do but does not always directly contribute to my objectives; red: does not help me achieve my objectives, or takes time away from my objectives).

4 Create an action plan to reduce your red tasks, manage time spent on your orange tasks, and take back time to add more time for green tasks.

Example:
Time Table

Hours per week	Task	Colour code	Comments	Actions
12	Reading and answering emails	Orange	Important to do but not always a good use of my time. Takes away from the time I spend with my team.	Limit time checking emails for one hour in the morning and one hour in the afternoon only Only answer the important emails – leave my team to answer the others Stop spending time filing emails into folders

Hours per week	Task	Colour code	Comments	Actions
4	Travelling to head office and back for meeting with my boss	Red	A lot of travel time for a one-hour meeting – and I can't use the time for working. I travel alone so can't spend the time catching up with my team.	Ask my boss if we can do the meeting via video conference instead, and advise that the time saved travelling can be spent on priority projects Arrange to travel with team members so that the time is not wasted, and can be spent catching up with each other
4	Digital transforma-tion project	Green	This is one of my most important projects and directly contributes to whether I get a bonus or not at the end of the year	Keep this time in the diary, and try to increase it by two hours per week for the whole team to get together and work on solutions

Hours per week	Task	Colour code	Comments	Actions
4	Impromptu meetings and discussions in the open plan office	Orange	Sometimes useful updates but more often just distractions, gossip and interruptions to my work. Unrelated to a specific project team	Tell people that morning that I am going to concentrate on a particular task, and wear headphones so I am not disturbed Book a meeting room to work in to avoid distractions Warn people that on Tuesdays and Wednesdays I am going to be 'un-distractable' to get on with work Be distractable on the other days of the week to join in with the office conversations

Hours per week	Task	Colour code	Comments	Actions
4	Lunch in the canteen with various team members	Green	Important to build relation-ships and have informal catch-ups – I often overhear something useful for my projects	Keep time booked in the diary for taking a lunch break, and make sure to choose different team members to sit with each day
3	Comms and marketing project team	Red	I know they want me there, but I don't need to be – I could ask for the agenda in advance, send my thoughts in advance via email, or only join for relevant sections	Contact the project team leader and explain I will contribute via email in advance of each meeting, and will send one of my direct reports once per week, but will no longer attend

Hours per week	Task	Colour code	Comments	Actions
3	One-to-one meetings with my two direct reports	Green	Very important as it helps me to prioritise their work and delegate to them	Prioritise these meetings, and use any saved time to do a catch-up with each direct report at the beginning and end of each week
2	HR catch-ups	Orange	Important meetings but not well planned	Reduce each meeting to 30 mins rather than an hour, and ask HR to send thoughts in advance, so the meeting is for decisions rather than catching up
1	Catch-up meeting with my boss	Green	Very important to manage their expectations	Prioritise this time, and keep what used to be travel time saved for preparing updates, quality thinking and ideas for this meeting

Tool 5

Meeting sharpeners

Time is our most valuable commodity, but we give it away so easily. If we want to spend more of our time at work getting our real work done, we need to say no to wasteful meetings.

A study in the UK in 2019 found that the average worker in the UK spends 26 working days in meetings, with an average of 20 minutes of a 60-minute meeting wasted due to lateness and technology not working. The study points to an epidemic of 'presenteeism', with more than 50% of respondents admitting to daydreaming during meetings rather than actively participating.[5]

As a team, agree how you will take control of your meetings by using any of the three meeting sharpeners:

- Do better meetings
- Meet less
- Cancel meetings

Do better meetings

- Use a memo system like Amazon (see example below). Develop a one-page memo structure that team members fill out in advance of the meeting. This details updates since the last meeting, key information and decisions for the team to discuss. All memos are compiled into one pre-read, so people are ready to discuss them. Often the discipline of writing this out helps people to prepare well, clarify their thoughts, and use the meeting time more wisely.

- Come with solutions. If someone wants to meet to ask the team's advice, ask them to come ready with at least two solutions to choose from. This makes them think through their question and answer in advance, using less time exploring the problem, and allowing more time for advice.

- Set up in advance. It seems obvious, but so much time is wasted in setting up meeting rooms and technology while the rest of the team watches the technical difficulties. Set up technology in advance so the team meeting is ready to start on time, have the different memos on the wall when people walk in for them to refer to, or if you really can't get into the meeting room to set it up, don't use technology at all, use printouts so no time is wasted on projectors and laptops.

- Walk and meet. For smaller meetings, go for a walk with someone instead of sitting for a meeting. This gives energy to the conversation and exercise too, maximising what you can get done in your available time – exercise and decision-making in one.

Amazon

Did you get the memo?

Jeff Bezos at Amazon has banned PowerPoint presentations in favour of memos. Before any meeting, the person who called the meeting submits a memo outlining what is to be discussed, information for decision-making and the outcomes that meeting wants. The meeting doesn't start until everyone has read the memo, even if it means waiting within the meeting for this to take place. This leads to better quality collaboration, because the person calling the meeting does the thinking first, rather than thinking out loud in a badly prepared meeting. It levels the playing field, making sure everyone starts with an informed view and can contribute immediately.

Example:
One-Page Memo

- -

Meeting name and date	Digital transformation meeting 17 June
Memo author	Pam Hamilton, MD
Topic	Decision to build pilot platform with one of two key suppliers
Decision required from the team	We have identified two potential platform suppliers with which to build our pilot platform. This memo details the strengths and weaknesses of each and asks for a decision on who to move forward with.
Key information for this decision	This section of the memo would outline the background, detail the strengths and weaknesses of each supplier, key dates milestones, budget implications of a decision in either direction, and the different decisions that can be made at this point, with a recommendation on which to go for
Supporting information	Where to read about this decision in more detail, attached files or links

Meet less

- If your regular meeting is normally an hour, consider making it 45 or even 30 minutes long. If you work with your team to make the agenda more efficient, they will appreciate the extra time they get back.

- As a team, agree on the most useful parts of the meeting agenda and consider where time could be reduced, for example:

    - Decide not to spend meeting time doing updates (people catching up since the last meeting) or downloads (presenting slides while people listen) in the meeting. Instead, send a pre-read in advance, and ask the team to come ready to respond, discuss or debate.

- Plan to meet face to face via video conference, rather than in person. This cuts down on everyone's travel time and on the possibility of people arriving late. Keep video cameras on to help people communicate better and stay focused.

- Start on time. Agree as a team that you will start on time and if people join late you won't stop and let them catch up. When people know time is limited, they tend to waste less time, arrive on time and get to the point quicker.

- Ask presenters to state the purpose of the presentation before they begin, what they want and need from those listening at the end, saving time on general discussion at the end and getting straight to the point.

Cancel meetings

- Say no to meetings that are not a good use of your time. This might challenge or even offend the meeting organiser at first, so be sure to respectfully explain why. This means they will value you more when you do attend and may change the way the meeting runs to make good use of your time to make you want to be there.

- Replace debriefs and updates with a pre-recorded video or podcast that people can watch or listen to at their convenience. With smartphones and laptop cameras it's relatively easy to record a dictation or a voice-over as you talk through the slides of a presentation. Send these out to the team rather than setting up a meeting to go through them in the same room at the same time.

- Ditch meetings that you half attend, half read emails in. If you can multi-task and don't contribute, you don't need to be there.

Tool 6

Email agreement

Sometimes it's easier to email than talk, but email can create a mass of work without leading to productivity. Agree with your team what is appropriate email etiquette and agree to stop email using up so much time and energy in your team.

You may find you need to do this with every new team you set up or join. Often people are frustrated with how much time they spend on email and will be delighted to set up some rules and expectations together to reduce their email burden.

Go through this ten-point checklist as a team to create your own email agreement:

1 **Don't email:** Are there times when we can phone each other rather than email? List them, even if obvious, and agree as a team to remind each other.

2 **Send texts or voicemails:** When is it better to send a text or a voicemail? Does everyone know how to send a voice-mail or a dictation?

3 **Reply now or later:** Decide between responding immediately to emails and coming back to them later. Storing up all your emails only to open them a second time to respond uses up time. Agree to try not to open emails twice if they can be dealt with on first reading.

4 **Chat group:** Can we create a WhatsApp or Slack group for conversations related to short projects that don't need long emails? What are our rules around sending these?

5 **Collect comments:** When an update needs to be emailed, and feedback collected, could we choose one person to receive individual comments and collate them on behalf of the group?

6 **Reply to all:** Can we agree not to use reply to all unless necessary? What are those times?

7 **24-hour answer:** Agree as a team that you will choose a limited amount of time in your day for emails, and agree not to answer emails outside of that time. Do we need to put on an out-of-office autoreply to let people know they won't get a response?

8 **Working hours:** If emails sent in non-working hours make people pressured to reply, can you schedule them to send in working hours? Or do you agree that people only need to answer in their own working hours?

9 **Stop filing:** Does your team need to spend time filing away emails into folders? If not, agree to store the most important, but leave the rest and search for them when needed.

10 **Digital workspace:** Can we use a project management system like Basecamp or Microsoft Teams for our project, where we store all files, actions, discussions and messages in one place? Do we agree to use this instead of sending each other files and meeting notes by email?

Example:
Completed Email Agreement

- -

Don't email	As a team we agree to only email when there are two or more people who need to be updated, and when the update is an important one for people to read and consider, or when commitments need to be recorded for future reference.
	We will talk to someone or phone them when we need to discuss something, rather than sending an email. We will have a fines jar for anyone who emails unnecessarily and will use it to fund a cake each month.

Send texts or voicemails	For questions that have a quick answer, we will send a text.
	For updates that need to be given but only need to be read once, we will send a voicemail or dictation, so we don't spend a long time composing an email that will only be read once.
Reply now or later	As a team we agree to try to open emails only once – responding there and then.
	For emails that need more attention, we will respond when we've had time to think, within 24 hours.
	If there's no easy reply and we need to discuss, we will talk. If we need to discuss as a group, we will add it to the agenda for our next meeting.
Chat group	We will use the team WhatsApp or Slack group instead of email for all quick updates and questions.
	We agree not to spam each other with messages like 'Thanks!' or emojis on the chat group.
Collect comments	When sending out information that needs comments and feedback, the person sending the email will collect individual comments and compile them, rather than everyone replying to all with feedback.
	Give the email a clear title and instruction so you know what is needed by when.
Reply to all	We agree as a team to ban 'reply to all' emails and will change our email settings to stop us from doing so as a default.
	If we need to make a comment or give feedback, we will do so to the person sending the email who will compile all responses.
	We give ourselves permission to remind people about the reply to all rule when they forget.

24-hour answer	We commit to spending one hour every day (and no more) catching up on emails.
	For each person this is a different time of day to suit them, but we acknowledge that emails will be responded to within 24 hours, so we will not expect immediate responses.
	We will use the chat group if we want an immediate response.
	We may choose to put on an out-of-office autoreply explaining that we will answer within 24 hours, or explaining the new email agreement until people get used to it.
Working hours	We will try to schedule sending emails only within working hours.
	If emails are sent outside of working hours, or people work at different times, we all agree that we are not expected to respond until we are at work ourselves.
Stop filing	Some important emails and documents need to be kept for future reference – we have asked one member of the team to store, archive and label these in a shared folder.
	For the rest of us, we agree not to spend any more time filing emails or documents.
Digital workspace	We will use a shared folder or digital workspace as a central space to store our actions, events, and files for the project.
	We agree to share all documents via this and not send emails with attachments anymore.

The time is now

Time is one of the most valuable and scarce resources we have. Supercharged teams prioritise where to focus their energy and resources to achieve their goals. Don't wait for permission, take back control of your team's time.

Key take outs

- -

- Create more time to be in your team by measuring where you spend and waste time.
- By becoming more efficient and selective about where we expend our effort, we can be more impactful.
- Stop spending so much time on emails by creating and sticking to a new email culture for your team.
- You can make meetings more effective and create more time for teamwork by sharpening them up.

chapter 4

What goals do you want to achieve?

Supercharged teams have a laser focus on a shared goal, and everything they do is in service of it. However, sometimes people *think* they're working towards the same goals, but either haven't agreed on them, or interpret the same goal differently.

If you've ever worked on projects that involve 'digital', 'sustainability' or 'personalisation', you will know that people use the same words to describe completely different things. To work together well, a team must clearly define their objective and work out the best way to achieve it. A crucial stage in supercharging your team is defining what successful outcomes look like. The tools in this chapter will give your team a clear and aligned direction so that you are all working towards the same goals.

What you will learn in this chapter:

- How to define the *outcomes* of your project, as well as the *outputs*

- How to create a powerful, compelling vision of what success looks like for your team
- How to ensure your team's objectives are motivating and understood by everybody in the same way

The difference between outputs and outcomes

In marketing projects, my objectives are output-based, with specific deliverables like ideas, innovations and decisions, but when I started working in the public sector, I heard people use the word 'outcomes'. The difference is that outputs are ideas, decisions and initiatives, and outcomes are what actually happen in people's lives as a result of the work.

When I interviewed Inspector Marcus Cator of the Hampshire Constabulary we talked about how the police set targets and plan what they want to achieve. Marcus told me that there has been a shift away from output-based policing targets (such as how many arrests are made) because arresting people does not always mean that the causes of crime are dealt with. Even though the police still need to solve crimes and arrest criminals, they have more outcome-based targets, such as addressing the causes of crime, keeping vulnerable people safe, and working with the wider community to share responsibility for keeping people healthy and happy so they don't find themselves in a situation where they turn to crime.

Tim Ferguson is CEO of Audience, and his team delivers big corporate events. He says if results are tangible and can be quantified, they are outputs. If they are attached to feelings or emotions, they are outcomes. Tim says that we can become fixated on the outputs (did we run to time, did we give all the updates we planned?), but forget the outcomes of such events (did we help them to develop stronger relationships with each other?). Tim says we must not underestimate the relevance of outcomes, such as trust and authenticity, as key drivers to outputs.[1]

In our teams, especially when we are under pressure, it can be easier to focus on the outputs and deliverables, without considering the outcomes. Outcomes are what can actually be achieved as a result of the team's work – they can be a more strategic view, or deliver culture change or impact in people's lives. Outcomes are often more emotional and motivating than outputs. I believe that a crucial stage in agreeing the team's ambition is defining what both the outcomes and outputs should be.

Envisioning success

Teamwork is the ability to work together toward a common vision. The ability to direct individual accomplishments toward organizational objectives. It is the fuel that allows common people to attain uncommon results.

Andrew Carnegie (1835–1919)

Visualisation has long been a part of elite sports: Team USA, the United States Olympic team, took nine sports psychologists to the 2014 Winter Olympics in Sochi.[2] Olympic athletes train to achieve peak physical performance, and they also train mentally for winning, by visualising what success looks and feels like. So powerful is visualisation that research has shown that it can improve physical performance whether or not the person visualising is also undertaking physical strength training.[3]

All supercharged teams envision their success. Visioning is a powerful way for a team to define what success looks and feels like, the possible positive outcomes that the team can create. If you focus first or only on the team's outputs and deliverables, you lose the potential to motivate your team with a wider purpose. When we create a positive vision of a successful future outcome, the outputs and deliverables fall into place.

The key to visioning success is to create an ambitious goal based on an idealistic vision, to help teams perform better. Education research has shown that if you have low expectations of someone, they will fail to achieve even those, whereas if you have high expectations of someone, they will meet if not exceed them. This is known as the Pygmalion or Rosenthal effect, and studies suggest that it is similarly impactful in the workplace.[4]

Teams that are clear on a shared vision excel, and those without a meaningful or clearly worded vision limit their performance.[5] Committing to goals improves performance, and if those goals are challenging and ambitious, they can raise performance levels, which is why at Google they deliberately set objectives that are ambitious and uncomfortable.[6] Setting ambitious, idealistic or uncomfortable goals is an excellent way to make your team want to achieve more, which means they do achieve more.

The HIVE Portsmouth

Visioning success

Volunteering is good for you. Research shows that volunteering is enjoyable, gives a sense of personal achievement, and makes people feel they are making a difference. Volunteers improve their wellbeing and feel less isolated.[7] So why don't more people do it? We know it is hard for volunteers to find the right opportunities to suit their skills and time, and part of this is not knowing what opportunities are available to them.

I led a visioning workshop on volunteering for residents and community groups in my local area. We asked people to draw the 'perfect world of volunteering'. It took a little time for people to warm up, but soon we had drawings of stick figures being active and connecting with each other and their community, and out and about in nature. At the centre of one of the pictures, someone had drawn a beehive and explained that the bees were people being busy, pollinating different flowers by sharing information, and the centre of that was a hive where everyone could come to be connected with each other and their community. In our perfect world of volunteering, people felt needed, sociable, full of energy, and the hive in the centre made that happen.

Out of this idealistic vision came the idea for a charity to share information across voluntary organisations, connect people with the right opportunities, and build that strong, happy and connected community. A year after that idealistic vision was created, the HIVE Portsmouth became the hub that coordinated the city's community response to the COVID-19 crisis, a response made possible by an army of local volunteers.

Great dreams aren't just visions, they're visions coupled to strategies for making them real.

Astro Teller[8]

Tool 7

Five futures

The five futures tool creates a successful vision of a project, supercharging it to drive optimism, energy and motivation towards a successful outcome. The key to any visioning exercise is to be ambitious, optimistic and idealistic at first. When a team creates what an incredibly positive future looks like, putting all their hopes, aspirations and emotions into that vision, they create their own 'moonshot', a term now used for very ambitious goals.[9]

Thinking about five years in the future when your team has been incredibly successful, choose one of these five questions to answer as a team:

1 What are the five best **outcomes** our team will have achieved? (These are the big, meaningful consequences that changed people's lives.)

2 What are the five best **ideas or initiatives** we will have created? (These are the specific things we have created – any great ideas, however wishful or impossible go here.)

3 Who are the five **people** who will have most benefited from our work and how? (These are the different types of customers, clients or residents we will help.)

4 What are the five most important **lessons** we will have learned as a team? (These are the ways of working that made our team great.)

5 How will our five most **successful decisions** have happened? (This is the journey the project took, and what we were able to overcome.)

The reason we ask for five is because it makes you go beyond the first few more obvious answers and stretches people's thinking to be far more ambitious. Visioning is a creative exercise for inspiration, not strategic alignment. Once the team has explored the optimistic possibilities and created possible outcomes, they can then use the Project navigator tool later in this chapter to agree on the specific outcomes and outputs of the team.

Other visioning techniques include creating a front page of a national newspaper in five years' time, or creating a perfect world as we did in the case study. Whatever the technique, putting people into a mindset of powerful future possibilities is incredibly motivating for a team.

Reframing your objective

When we define our team's objectives, people use the same language to mean very different things. The bigger the topic, the broader the subject, the more I have found that people assume they mean the same thing when they don't. This means that for the hardest topics we make the worst assumptions.

A case in point is overuse of the word 'digital'. In a report commissioned with industry leaders, nine out of ten companies surveyed claimed they were undergoing digital transformation, even though only a quarter of them admitted to knowing what it was.[10] Digital transformation means different things to different people,[11] and what is ironic is what holds back digital transformation really comes down to culture and people, rather than digital skills.[12]

So, while we might start with an objective like 'To digitally transform our company', a reframed objective that would achieve a more successful outcome could be 'To help the people in our company embrace new digital ways of working'. The first is based around the topic (digital transformation), and while it may be accurate, it is a limited, basic view of the objective and does not help us move towards a solution. The second is better because it is richer and helps to frame the importance of people in achieving a successful outcome (helps people change their attitude to digital transformation).

In his book *Who do you want your customers to become?* Michael Schrage talks about 'The Ask': how successful companies reframe their objective in terms of how they want their customer to evolve. So like Starbucks, who wanted customers to become discerning coffee drinkers, or Google, who wanted its users to become partners and collaborators in finding information, companies can achieve huge success by considering what they want their future customers to experience, believe or become.

Tool 8

Reframe your aim

Ask a boring question, get a boring answer. Ask a motivating question, get a motivating answer. And if you can ask a supercharged question, you are more likely to create a supercharged answer. This tool is about rewording your

---

team's objective in a way that makes it more meaningful, more inspiring and more ambitious.

As a team, reframe your project objective by creating new versions through these lenses:

1 Reword the objective as if you were explaining it to a five-year-old child or an alien from another planet.

2 Reword the objective as if you were a well-known company or personality.

3 Reword the objective as if you had all the money or resources in the world.

4 State the objective as if you had no money or no resources.

Once you've collected your reframed and reworded objectives, choose the best wording and frames to create one powerful, reframed aim for your team.

Example:
Reframe Your Aim

Original objective: To Digitally Transform Our Company

Five-year-old child	To help everyone learn how to use computers and the internet better so that we can beat the robots
Alien from another planet	To help humans to communicate their culture and intelligence into the future and explore life beyond earth
Well-known company (Netflix)	To deepen the emotional experience our people feel when digital technology helps them

Well-known personality (Margaret Attwood)	To free workers from the slavery of routine tasks and unnecessary mental load, so that they have more time to dedicate to fighting injustice and creating better lives
All the money	To give every single person in the company the highest spec digital makeover to give them every technological enhancement possible
All the resources	To teach every employee everything they need to deeply understand and learn everything that technology has to offer them in their work
No money	Tell everyone they have to teach themselves how to transform their own job to be more digital, or leave the company
No resources	Switch off all non-digital communication tomorrow and let people catch up if they can themselves
Important reframed angles	Communicating culture and intelligence
	Deeper emotional experiences
	Freedom from slavery and drudgery
	Digital enhancement
	Teach themselves
Final reframed aim	To perform a deep digital makeover for every individual in the company so they can experience the benefits of a successful digital transformation at first hand

Project scoping

Some of the biggest failures are projects where the project scope was not fully agreed, or changed massively after it had started. I once did a three-month innovation project for a toothpaste brand, creating a new six-point benefits checklist, new ingredients and benefits to sell a premium innovation. At our debrief, the senior stakeholder was disappointed. He said that what he had really wanted at the beginning of the project was an innovation that would create a new red pack to stand out on a shelf. Unfortunately, he hadn't told us that.

To help avoid just such a situation, successful companies like Unilever use a scoping template that follows the same structure for all projects, and is signed off by all team members and stakeholders before the project gets underway.

Tool 9

Project navigator

Building on all the best scoping tools and templates from the different teams I've worked in, here are the main points your team must align on at the beginning of a project – and keep coming back to as the project evolves. Even agreeing on the journey so far can be important. The story people tell has a huge influence on the approach your team takes. Feel free to use the business terms in the second column if more appropriate.

Journey so far	Context	The reason we are here today, what has happened so far to get us here, the context of the market, the background of the team or business and why this is more important now than it was before
Destination	Objective	The end goal of our project or team, what's in it for us and what will we create or make happen as a result
Guides	Assumptions	We are guided by these beliefs, values and assumptions

Gifts	Resources	The talents, powers, resources, time, people, tool and budget we have for this journey
Roadmap	Plan	Where we plan to go, how we will get there and the timing of our journey
Traps	Out of scope	Where we will not go, risks we will avoid and where we won't spend our time or attention
Treasure	Outputs	What we aim to create or find, the prize of success, what we plan to win or achieve and what we will deliver
Destiny	Outcome	What this journey means, how this journey will make the world a better place, the possible future we will create when we get this right and the ideal outcome

Make your goal big and clear

The best teams work towards a singular goal, and the most ambitious goals inspire the best results. Going beyond a basic business objective to align on a project ambition that creates successful outcomes and then scoping the team's work well is the foundation for a supercharged team to achieve success.

Key take outs

- The human benefits (outcomes) of your project are as important to the success of your team as the business objectives (outputs).
- Your team will achieve more if they are working towards ambitious goals based on a compelling vision of success.
- Properly scoping your project and agreeing clear objectives that are understood by everybody in the same way are key to delivering a project that achieves its goals.

chapter 5

Find your motivation

Supercharged teams are driven to succeed by a strong motivation for achieving their goal. Even when you have a clear vision for your team, teamwork can be challenging without the motivation to do the work. With a strong purpose, a team will be far more motivated to achieve more together. For some teams, their organisation's greater purpose will provide all the motivation they need, even if the work they are doing is difficult. For some people, they are driven by a kind of reactor core that keeps them going long after the rest of us will have given up and acts as a filter for all decisions. Internal drive and motivation are crucial – we cannot supercharge without them.

Use these tools to ramp up the meaning and purpose of your work for yourself and your team.

What you will learn in this chapter:

- How to motivate your team by having a purpose.
- How to reveal and articulate your team's purpose.
- How to deepen your understanding of why the team's work matters.
- How individual team members can find their motivation.

Purpose motivates teams

Organizations are focusing not only on being a great place to be, but also to be from.

Global Talent Trends 2019.[1]

Of the many interviews I did for this book, almost every person mentioned the importance of purpose at work. Grainne Wafer from Diageo said that the best way to be a successful team is to have clarity of purpose – a true understanding of what you are doing and why you are doing it, so the team is clear what they are in service of. Gael De Talhouet from Essity said the best teams don't succeed because they work harder or longer, but succeed because of the passion they share and their motivation to exceed expectations.

More and more companies understand that if people's work actually stands for something, the more motivated and effective their teams will be. In the last ten years we have seen a remarkable shift in what customers expect. It is not enough simply to be profitable – organisations have to stand for something and to contribute something to society.[2] This is partly because it is harder for companies to hide unethical behaviour, so they have to behave better. It is also because customers have more choice than before, and one way that companies can stand out is by doing good. Today, people want to buy and work for brands that reflect their own values.

This is the same for employers – people want to work somewhere that does good work. In 2014, KPMG's 'Higher Purpose' initiative recognised and celebrated the impact and meaning of the work the company did. It found that when its leaders communicated the higher purpose and impact of their work, their teams were significantly more motivated to strive for continuous improvement and high performance.[3]

When companies can form a human connection with their employees and build trust and pride in what they do, they improve the performance of their people. In other words, when work is meaningful, teams perform better.

Diageo

How gender is communicated in advertising

I've worked on many projects over the last two decades, and only a few stand out. The ones that do are those with a strong social purpose. One of the best projects I've ever been a part of was with Diageo, one of the world's biggest producers of spirits and beers.

Diageo is a leading company for inclusion and diversity. In 2020 it was featured in the Bloomberg Gender-Equality Index for the third year running,[4] and in 2019 named the second most inclusive and diverse company in the world by Refinitiv,[5] and ranked first globally for gender equality by Equileap as a result of this work.[6]

Diageo is responsible for advertising hundreds of recognisable brands, and in 2018, Syl Saller, the Chief Marketing Officer, kicked off a purpose-based initiative to normalise gender equality. Syl believes passionately that advertising shapes culture – what people see on screen has an influence on how we behave in society. Historically, women have been misrepresented in advertising. For example, in mixed gender adverts generally, men speak about seven times more than women,[7] and in Diageo's own advertising male voiceovers had historically been more common than female-only voiceovers.

Amber D'Albert in my team led the work with Diageo to improve gender portrayal in advertising, working with the business to produce a framework for progressive gender portrayal that Diageo's 1,200 marketeers, global and local agencies were trained in. Diageo has shared this framework widely with the industry, including the Unstereotype Alliance.

When we worked on this project, we deliberately selected an all-female team, including our designer, so that the 'female gaze' led every element. Because of the purpose, we were motivated to do our best ever award-winning work. Imagine the societal impact that one of the world's biggest advertisers will have on gender equality.

Employees don't need to work at your company, they should want to work there and as a result everything should be designed around that principle.

Jacob Morgan[8]

Tool 10

Define team purpose

We don't all belong to an organisation with ambitions to change the world. However, if you want to supercharge your team, no matter what you aim to achieve, you can create a team purpose that powerfully drives the team to keep you going when the work is tough.

In the previous chapter your team will have created a vision, the ambitious direction for your team. The team's purpose is *why* you are doing what you do. To find your team's purpose, you need to define why you are doing this work, and that reason will give your team the passion and energy, the reactor core, that makes them exceed expectations.

Once you have your goal, consider these six questions in turn, as a team, to define your team's purpose:

1 Starting with the team vision you created in the previous chapter, what is your one-sentence expression of this team vision?

2 What unique talent and expertise does this particular team have to achieve this vision?

3 What are the assumptions and beliefs we bring to this project?

4 Based on the previous three answers, why do we exist and therefore what is our team's purpose?

5 With our team's purpose in mind, how will we overcome challenges that come our way?

6 With our team's purpose in mind, how will we make progress?

Answer these six questions to arrive at six short sentences or statements that define your team's purpose and how it will help you to achieve your team vision.

Example:
Define Team Purpose

Purpose questions	Example answers from the digital transformation team (from the previous chapter)
One-sentence vision	To perform a deep digital makeover for every individual in the company so they can experience the benefits of a successful digital transformation at first hand.
Talents and expertise	We are ten of the top digital experts in the business, with experience from inside and outside of the company. If we can't do it, literally nobody can.

Purpose questions	Example answers from the digital transformation team (from the previous chapter)
Assumptions and beliefs	We are convinced that digital transformation will make work easier, more efficient and more enjoyable for every single person in the company, and will have a positive impact on their work–life balance. This project will make people's lives better.
Our team's purpose	We exist to make people's work easier and better with digital tools that save time, enable great work and help people to have a better work–life balance.
Overcoming our challenges	We know that people resist change, and we need to remember to prove to people that this will actually be better for their overall work–life balance, not just their work. We will have to convince them gently, one person at a time.
Making progress	We will identify individuals who will find digital transformation easiest, work with them first, and ask them to talk about the benefits to both their work and home life to others in the company, and ask them to help other people overcome their issues.
	We will work to understand those individuals with the most barriers, difficulties or challenges to working digitally, and understand what benefits will make a difference to them (for example, allowing people to work flexibly and from home) and focus on delivering them these benefits first.

How to use this tool:

- Ask each person in the team to write their answers to these questions on Post-it notes first, individually and without discussion, and using the most descriptive language possible.

- When everyone has finished answering the first question, only then share the notes with each other, and agree one main answer taking the best bits from all of them.

- Then move to answering the next question in the same way.

- Don't stop at defining your team's purpose, but move beyond to what that means for dealing with challenges, and how you will make progress.

- Make your answers emotional, descriptive and colourful – the more memorable and meaningful they are, the more motivating they will be.

Your team's purpose should be relevant in the short and medium term, but when you create a purpose at the beginning of the project, you may find it needs to change once the project is underway. So, after the early stages of your team's work are done, sense-check the team's purpose, and reword it if necessary.

Purposeful leadership works

Put simply, the way people feel at work profoundly influences how they perform.

Schwartz et al[9]

Whether or not your organisation has a strong purpose, it is important to motivate your team to want to do great work. Purposeful leadership is growing in importance in today's workplace. Extensive research has found that when managers display 'purposeful' behaviours, employees are less likely to quit, they are more satisfied and willing to go the extra mile, they are better performers and less cynical, proving 'the modern workplace is as much a battle for hearts and minds as it is one of rules and duties'.[10]

A strong purpose can motivate our bosses too. John Monks is a leadership coach who works to help creative leaders achieve their full potential. When we talked, he told me that he is seeing the evolution of purpose in brands for individual leaders who need to find how their own values and interests can be aligned with their work. Doing this helps them navigate the complexity and pace of today's world, alongside a desire to take control of the creative process.

Kantar

Purposeful collaboration

One of the first people I interviewed for this book was Beth Ann Kaminkow, at that time CEO of Kantar Consulting. Kantar is a data, insights and consulting company with over 30,000 employees working in a hundred different countries. In a business like this, because they are working on lots of different projects, teams can sometimes compete with each other instead of working together for their clients. Beth Ann and her leadership team developed an initiative called 'purposeful collaboration' to encourage teams to work together better across departments.

Kantar looked at high potential collaborators who were already doing great work, and developed a set of principles and a new way to kick off projects. Every project started by identifying the purpose of the project (the client question), the outcome (what they aimed to achieve together), the team (who would collaborate on this) and only after that defined the scope, timing and budget. This was so that people weren't being pulled into anything and everything under the guise of 'collaboration'.

This gave new meaning to everyone's work, with inspiration and expertise from a wider pool of collaborators, and more successful projects because clients were getting the richness and depth of knowledge Kantar is known for. As a cross-company effort it made people feel like they were having a greater impact, something that would not have been possible in the siloed departments of the past. Beth Ann told me that it led to positive business and people results, driving 'higher client value, engagement and satisfaction, and creating a virtuous cycle of employee engagement and motivation'. Purposeful collaboration is now a core value at Kantar, which is a huge achievement given the size and scale of the company.

Tool 11

Why our work matters

People get a sense of purpose from feeling connected to something bigger than themselves, knowing their work matters and understanding how their work affects other people.[11] This tool helps your team to be more aware of the work and its positive impact, linking the team's work with the greater good it can do beyond the team.

If you work only for yourself, if you hit rock bottom, you give up, but if you work for other people you can never give up because it becomes a bigger cause.

Kelly Choi[12]

As a team, with your team purpose in mind, consider the positive impact that the team could make. Answer these questions together to inspire and motivate each other about the work you are doing as a team. You can visualise these as if building a pyramid, starting with the base and building upwards.

1 How will the company benefit from the work this team is doing?

2 What positive impact will this team have on the people in different departments or other parts of the organisation?

3 How will our work benefit people outside of the company?

4 How will this work have a positive impact on our family and friends?

5 What will our work give to our community or local area?

Example:
Why Our Work Matters

- -

Our team's purpose is that we exist to make people's work easier and better with digital tools that save time, enable great work and help people to have a better work–life balance.

Our work matters because:

1 The work this team does will make the business more efficient, and will give us the tools and time we need to be better than our competitors.

2 This work will have a positive impact on everyone in the organisation, in every department, because we will make their lives easier, make their work–life balance better, and make them enjoy working here more than before.

3 The work this team does will be an example of brilliant digital transformation, and we will inspire other traditional companies to make this change for the good of their business and employees.

> **4** Our work will be good for our friends and family because they will notice we are spending more time with them, and we will do such a great job that we will be promoted and earn more money to share with them.
>
> **5** As a result of this work, we will have more time to work in and volunteer in our community as a result of the free time we've made, and more money to spend in the local economy.
>
> By considering how our work affects others, it reminds us who we are helping and how, in big and small ways, and in direct and indirect ways. This tool helps you to identify and remember what matters about your team's work, and why the work is important.

Motivation is crucial to mental health

Everything can be taken from a man but one thing: the last of the human freedoms – to choose one's attitude in any given set of circumstances, to choose one's own way.

Victor Frankl (1905–97)

Psychologists have found that a sense of purpose enhances our self-esteem and self-confidence as long as we feel we are moving successfully towards our goals. Having purpose can also make us less focused on our own anxieties and worries because we feel a part of something bigger.[13] People with a purpose in life also live longer.[14]

However, for many of us being in a team is not a choice – you have to be there, told to be there, even if you don't want to be. You might be working with people you don't like, on a project you don't believe in, in a company you are not proud of. When you find yourself in this situation, it can be quite serious, as a lack of meaning and purpose in your work makes you less motivated and less happy.

If possible, try to find some meaning and purpose in where you are and the team you are in, even if you are not currently enjoying it. This is your chance to find something in that team that keeps you going.

Finding your personal motivation

When I was 25, I moved to London from Zimbabwe. Immigrants often have to start from scratch in a new country, so even though I had marketing experience, I started off working as a hotel reception-ist for a few months, before getting an admin job at Kraft Foods. I knew Kraft was a good company to work for, and I thought that if I did a great job there might be more opportunities for me. On my first day I was shown into a large boardroom with hundreds of boxes in it, piled almost to ceiling height. Inside was the company paperwork from the last 20 years, and my job was to archive the important records and shred everything else. I worked my way through all the boxes eight hours a day for three months – that's almost 500 hours of filing.

As I worked, I kept the door open and greeted the other people in the office as they walked past, and found out as much as I could about what the company did, and who people were. When the archiving project was over and the boardroom was clear of boxes, I threw away my plastic finger protectors and asked if they had any other work for me. That's how I met my first boss and mentor Monica Juanas, and gained the consumer insight which became the founda-tion of my career.

No matter what work you are doing, it is important to feel your work is worth it. Whether the company does great work that you can be a part of, or if you have to find your own meaning and motivation to keep going, when you have a good reason for doing your work, the work will feel better.

Working hard for something we don't care about is called stress: Working hard for something we love is called passion.

Simon Sinek[15]

Tool 12

Personal motivators

This tool recognises that you may not be in the team of your dreams, but being in a team is hardly ever a life sentence. We can check our own mindset and find the benefits to keep us motivated by asking how we can benefit from this work or team, despite its difficulties.

Please note, if you are being bullied, or the work your team is doing is unethical or illegal, you must reach out for support rather than using this tool.

Assuming you can accept the team you are in and want to make the best use of the experience that you can, here are some personal motivation questions you can ask yourself to find a few ways of finding motivation even in a difficult working situation:

- Does this team open you up to new opportunities in the future? Is this work a stepping stone to other teams or projects? What do you need to get out of this experience to make your next move possible?

- Is there a specific area of expertise, topic or skill you can learn while part of the team? Is there a new responsibility and opportunity to learn, for example, taking meeting minutes or setting up a project management system?

- Is there a person on the team you admire or aspire to be like? Could you watch them and learn from them? What do they do in tricky situations that you could apply to your own

---

ways of working? What example do they set and how can you learn from them?

- Can you learn about team dynamics, management or relationships while you participate in this team? Are there any books you can read to understand why the different team players act like they do? Is there someone in the team who can help explain it to you, so you understand more deeply why we work in this way?

Then reflect on what you have learnt:

- Reflect on your own career, what you aspire to achieve, and how you will get there, including what you commit to doing and to never doing, based on the behaviours you see around you.

- Make an effort to empathise with people in the team, understanding more deeply why they are behaving in a certain way, being sympathetic to their pressures and mistakes and offering acceptance and support.

- Consider your escape plan or alternatives – where would you like to be, and how do you plan to get there?

- Understand why – learn from the people around you, even if how not to do things.

Write about it:

- Can you record, measure or code what is happening in the team, observing what is happening and analysing it to identify specific patterns? For example, recording how many minutes late each meeting starts, and total these up for all meetings in the year to show how your team can improve. Or recording how long one person talks versus the others in the team, and creating a comparison of airtime over time.

- Can you record the story of this team as an interesting case study to teach other people about in a future role?

- Can you write a private blog or journal about your experiences that you can turn into an article, book or comedy in future?

Have fun with it:

- Create harmless experiments, competitions and games to enjoy the time you spend in the team, for example, writing yourself a bingo sheet of commonly used phrases to tick off, or making it your mission to make sure people have to sit in a new chair each time by moving in each meeting. My husband once spent a year's worth of meetings with a large cost-cutting consultancy group taking their paper clips from them when they weren't looking, building up a collection that he was very proud of.

Reach out to others:

- Reach out for support, whether to a coach, leader, boss, your HR person or a peer, and ask for them to help you find personal motivation and benefits in this team, even if the work feels difficult or unmotivating at first glance.

- Can you use the benefit of your experience to reach out to more junior colleagues and help to grow the next generation of leaders? Helping others can be hugely motivating in itself.

Motivation is essential

Whatever we do, and whichever team we are in, we can supercharge it by finding a deeper motivation to do our work. Even the best teams face challenges and difficulties, and it's the internal drive that keeps us going together. Our motivation is the reason why we get out of bed in the morning and come to work. It's far beyond and more important than selling more products, hitting deadlines or making money.

When a team has a purpose, they have defined why their work is meaningful, and why they are so motivated to do that work. A motivated team feels better to be in and works better too. Finding your motivation is crucial to doing excellent teamwork.

Key take outs

- -

- Purpose is a strong motivator, and motivated teams perform better.
- Defining a team's purpose will help find the passion and energy to exceed expectations.
- Understanding why the team's work matters connects them to something bigger than themselves.
- Finding personal motivations within your work can help you make the best of challenging situations.

chapter 6

Agree what you will deliver, and when

Supercharged teams have highly motivated team members who are chosen to make a difference and are ready for action. When your team's ambition is clear and you've found your motivation, you will be keen to get started. I'm the kind of person who prefers to get going than to think too long and hard about how to get somewhere. However, before you leap into teamwork, it is important to agree on what the team will deliver, and by when. A supercharged team deliberately decides how fast they will work, the deadlines they will set, and what success looks like.

As a team you need to be relentlessly focussed on your goal, but not so rigid that you don't allow time to reflect or pivot if necessary. This chapter will help you to design your project journey with your goals in mind, in order to make the best use of your team's time, with the momentum and pace you need to get there. Whether your team is midway through a project, or about to start a new one, supercharge your roadmap with these tools.

What you will learn in this chapter:

- How to plan your project journey.
- How to avoid the perils of 'press-on-itis'.
- How to keep up the pace and avoid burnout.
- How to create time and space for reflection.
- How to use pilots and prototypes to achieve better outcomes.
- How to measure success.

Plan your journey

It is more important to know where you are going than to get there quickly.

Mabel Newcomer (1892–1983)

Even if your team has a very clear destination in mind, you do need to plan your journey. In 2010, a British man bought a motor boat on the internet and set off on what he intended to be a round-Britain trip by sea, armed with a road map and a radio he didn't know how to use. He set off from the Thames, aiming for Southampton, reasoning that he could motor out to sea and keep the land on his right until he got there. He travelled for a day and a half and ran out of fuel before he realised that he had been circling the Isle of Sheppey rather than travelling west. Coastguard Ian Goodwin said with typical British understatement, 'We passed on relevant safety advice and advised him that the best way to Southampton would be by train'.[1]

It's a funny story and we probably believe we would never set off on a journey with only a destination in mind and no plan for how to get there. However, I do often see teams set off towards a big goal with just a list of actions and dates, without truly considering the shape of the journey and how they will track their progress.

My husband Paul is a sailor and a pilot, and every time I travel with him I'm impressed by the amount of time he spends planning how to navigate each journey before the journey starts. Like anyone in a high-risk job, he wouldn't dream of setting off without considering weather conditions, traffic, permissions, our equipment, the vessel itself and any risks (including the competence of his crew – that's me!). Even after all that planning, we do sometimes find ourselves in some big storms or contrary tides out on the Solent. A navigation plan predicts possible challenges, and it plans to overcome them to get to the destination safely. A huge part of being safe is being able to tell at any point in the journey whether you are on track or not.

Andrew Grove, author of *High Output Management,* talks about 'management by objectives' – knowing where I want to go (my objective) and how I will pace myself to see if I'm getting there (milestones or key results). He says that the milestones must provide feedback on the journey so far, no matter where we are, so we can make adjustments if we are not on track.[2]

Tool 13

The journey plan

Perhaps you are in a pretty straightforward team and you're not planning on a huge adventure. However, you do have an opportunity to supercharge the journey by considering how your journey might look and what challenges you may face. You can better plan to get to your destination.

There are four stages in creating a journey plan:

1 Define your destination clearly.

2 Consider the challenges you are likely to face.

3 Plan the route you will take to get there.

4 Identify milestones and signposts to track your progress.

Define your destination clearly

If you don't know where you're going, you will not get there.

Andrew Grove[3]

In the previous chapter, your team created a broad goal. In our example this was 'To perform a deep digital makeover for every individual in the company so they can experience the benefits of a successful digital transformation at first hand'. In order to make this into a clear destination, we now need to define it more specifically.

Psychologists have found that having a clearly articulated, specific goal significantly boosts productivity and performance because clear goals focus our attention, help us to stay on track and encourage us to be persistent.[4] A simple formula for a proper goal was created by John Doerr, venture capitalist and author of *Measure What Matters*, as follows: '*I will _____ as measured by _____.*'

A goal must describe what you will achieve and how you are going to measure that achievement.[5] Our adventurer on his way to Southampton had a wish rather than a goal. Any sailor knows that you need to have planned where you will dock, so a true goal would have been a specific mooring at Town Quay Marina in Southampton, supported by a passage plan of how to get there safely.

Our first step as a team is making a broad goal more specific, which involves breaking it down into important measurable parts, as follows:

- We will perform a deep digital makeover for all 200 individuals in the company.

- We will create a personalised plan for each individual's current digital use, barriers to overcome and possible benefits to them through our project.

- We will conduct a satisfaction survey to compare how they feel at work, their working patterns and work–life balance, pre- and post-digital transformation.

- We will deliver digital transformation to every individual, until every person in the company is using at least one new digital device, technology or programme in their job on a regular basis.

- We will know we have succeeded when by 31 December, at least 90% of people have experienced some benefit as a result of the transformation, as measured by our survey.

Once you have a clear destination in mind, you can see what will help you get there, or stand in your way.

Consider the challenges you are likely to face

In his book *The Culture Code,* Daniel Coyle talks about imagining what could get in the way of your goal and looking at other teams to see how they overcame similar obstacles. In most projects you should have a good idea of the kinds of challenges you might face, such as team members being swamped with workload at a busy time of year, or a board meeting that will decide whether your project gets funding or not. Think through the likely challenges your project will face, and when they are likely to happen list them out against your specific goal.

Example:
Consider the challenges you are likely to face

Specific goal	Challenges we may face
We will perform a deep digital makeover for all 200 individuals in the company	Staff turnover means that 20% of these will join at some point during the year, so we need to consider how to do this with new joiners, even if they join in December
We will create a personalised plan for each individual's current digital use, barriers to overcome and possible benefits to them through our project	People could be reluctant to be honest about how and when they work – no one wants their work to be scrutinised by a different department
We will conduct a satisfaction survey to compare how they feel at work, their working patterns and work–life balance, pre- and post-digital transformation	We won't know the right questions to ask before we have created personalised plans – so designing the pre-transformation measures will be difficult
We will deliver digital transformation to every individual, until every person in the company is using at least one new digital device, technology or programme in their job on a regular basis	Before we begin the project, it's hard to know whether this is possible or completely over-ambitious. What about if we find that there is one team who simply cannot do anything more digitally in their jobs?
We will know we have succeeded when by 31 December at least 90% of people have experienced some benefit as a result of the transformation, as measured by our survey	We need to be careful about how we design the survey – in case people disagree with how we measure 'some benefit'

At this point, don't worry about solving the challenges, simply list them out as a team. As anyone who has done a risk assessment will tell you, just talking about the risks will make you more aware of what you need to consider before you embark on your project plan.

Plan the route you will take to get there

You have your clear destination in mind, and you are aware of the challenges you may face. Now combine these into an idea of how the project journey might look through the year. A simple way to do this is to plot a 'roadmap' on a big wall, or an Excel spreadsheet if you prefer, showing the months of the year from left to right. Start by plotting the specific goals first on the far-right column that represents your deadline. Then work back from each goal to establish when certain things need to happen in the year, keeping in mind the challenges.

Using our example, if we focus on the specific goal 'We will know we have succeeded when by 31 December at least 90% of people have experienced some benefit as a result of the transformation, as measured by our survey', with the challenge 'We need to be careful about how we design the survey – in case people disagree with how we measure "some benefit" in mind.'

We can work back from our goal, with the challenges in mind, like this.

December	90% of the people surveyed believe that our project was of benefit to them in their work
November	100% of people have completed the survey, and results are analysed
October	Heads of department and CEO launch the post-transformation survey and ask people to complete it
September	Project team offers mentoring and further training for individuals or departments who need it

August	Project team designs and delivers training to each department in their new digital tools
July	Based on the pilots, each department agrees at least one new digital approach they commit to being trained on
June	Departments pilot new digital tools and work out which ones make work easier
May	Project team identifies technology and programmes to deliver the benefits people have identified in the survey
April	Project team analyses survey results and works out the key areas per department where digital could improve their work
March	Project team sends out a pre-transformation survey based on the feedback from the department meetings, including specific benefits that people would like to see in their jobs by December
February	Heads of departments cascade the digital transformation plan to their teams, asking for them to be involved and reinforcing the benefits to them. Collect from each team the kinds of benefits they would hope for from digital transformation in their job.
January	The CEO announces the company digital transformation plan and the aim of making people's work–life balance better as a result

When you focus on each of your destination points in turn, and work back through the year, you will start to see where there may be problems, stresses or difficulties as the activities overlap and cause issues. For example, if the company-wide training is planned for August, but most people are on holiday, you may need to speed up the earlier stages.

Once you've completed this for every goal, you will see the amount of activity your team has to plan for, and the journey of the project, month by month.

Having a plan, feeling confident and being competent are the greatest antidotes to fear. If you're just trying to deal with the unknown by crossing your fingers and hoping, you will be utterly helpless when a situation finally manifests. . . You need to take ownership of a situation, break it down into bitesize chunks and plan accordingly.

Chris Hadfield[6]

Identify milestones and signposts to track your progress

Your team will now have a big map that outlines all of the key tasks that will happen through the year to deliver all the destination points. Now we need to work out how to measure whether we are on or off track. Of course, in regular team meetings to check on the project's progress, but we need to be able to tell where we are and make adjustments to avoid going off course.

To go back to our man travelling to Southampton, we need to identify specific points along the journey that he recognises, so he knows he is going in the right direction, such as passing Portsmouth's Spinnaker Tower before he gets to Southampton, and crucially what he will do if he doesn't see the Spinnaker Tower after travelling for over a day.

Organise your project journey into key milestones (important stages in the journey) and how you will measure progress at each point.

Quarter 1: Launch and cascade	Board members have approved the digital transformation plan and have booked dates with their teams for the cascade sessions. There is a company-wide buzz and excitement, although some departments are less enthusiastic than others.
Quarter 2: Digital investigation	We are working on multiple investigations into new digital tools and have already identified one or two key pilots and departments to trial
Quarter 3: Digital training	Teams are talking to each other about the training and encouraging each other to go on it, although some departments are trickier than others to get the training booked in because of workload
Quarter 4: Assessing project success	Most departments have had their training and are using the new technology, so now we need to get people talking about the benefits to encourage each other

Once you've identified where you should be at each stage of the journey, it is far easier to know if you are not on track and adjust your journey at that point. It is especially important for longer term projects to keep adapting to fit new leaders, new market conditions, or new customer needs. If by the end of Quarter 2 you have not identified the right digital tools to train people in, you may need to push the training to later in the year.

Along with milestones, think through signposts with your team – the things that you see along the journey that give you warnings or encouragement. In my experience with working on big, company-wide projects, one important signpost that shows you are heading in the right direction is when someone gets cross about the project because they feel they have been left out. The fact that they want to join your team's journey is a good thing and can be a great opportunity to get more people on side.

In my years of leading innovation projects, we knew that there were two signposts that were the death knell of any new product. If at any time a consumer said 'I like this, it would be good for a picnic' or 'This would be good to take on holiday' we knew that we should just stop the project right there and go home. When consumers think they like a product but can't imagine using it in everyday life, it's time to call quits on that innovation.

The Show Must Go Online

Imitation is a good sign

Another signpost of success is being imitated. Robert Myles and Sarah Peachey created The Show Must Go Online in response to COVID-19. The idea was to perform all of Shakespeare's plays live via Zoom in the order in which they are believed to have been written. Within a week they broadcast their first show, with 730 people watching them performing live via YouTube, and more than 10,000 views in three days. In just eight weeks, major media outlets across the world had covered them in over 40 articles, including the UK, US, Australia, Singapore, India, Russia and more, with over 100,000 views combined.

Rob says that imitation is the sincerest form of flattery. Over 20 theatre companies, drama schools and universities reached out for advice on how to replicate the success of the show, with others, from one-person operations to national institutions, replicating certain features of the broadcasts, even down to the wording.[7]

Avoiding press-on-itis

Press-on-itis is the official name given to a well-documented human error that occurs in airplane accidents, also called 'goal fixation' or 'hurry syndrome. Pilots go against advice or data, and continue on even when safer alternatives exist, such as trying to land again and again, even if the weather hasn't improved, or racing ahead of a thunderstorm to try to beat it home. Press-on-itis accounts for 42% of landing accidents and serious incidents in aviation.

The types of pilots who suffer the most from this are those who have the most professional pride and want to give superior service for the company and its customers.[8] Project teams, especially the ones who are trying their best to make a project successful, can fall into the same trap. When we are working in a team, sometimes the very fact that we've been working on something for so long means we are even more likely to keep pressing on with it, in spite of ever mounting difficulties.

However, many successful teams agree that stopping the wrong project is just as important as starting the right ones. Trying to do too many projects or working ad hoc projects can dilute your team's effectiveness.[9] When your project journey becomes difficult, and all the signposts are telling you to stop, you may need to consider doing so.

You need a 'stop sign'. . . . It's OK to put a stop to some things.
Benchmarking Innovation Impact[10]

It is hard to put a stop on projects that are failing if we work in a culture that fears failure. Shalaka Karandikar is a Senior Innovation Manager at Lloyds Banking Group, and she says it is important to encourage a culture of learning by encouraging people to share successes and ways in which they failed fast through experimentation. In her project goals, she instils the acceptance of both success and failure by identifying hypotheses to disprove, or identifying how much money will be saved if a project is stopped early enough.

To avoid press-on-itis, we must keep a lookout for signs that tell us to stop or pivot. Eric Ries, author of *The Lean Startup*, coined the term 'pivot': the idea that successful startups change directions but stay grounded in what they've learned. Lessons may be learned from the project so far, and work may be repurposed, but if the project is becoming a wasted effort rather than progressing, it is time to cast aside the original plan and work towards a new goal.

A great example of this is Thai Airways' pivot to encourage travellers to stay at home during the coronavirus pandemic. In order to support social distancing and people staying at home, they rewarded members of their loyalty scheme free miles to stay at home. To be validated, members download an app which uses geolocation technology to determine their location. From a company who encouraged people to travel more, the pivot was significant, though temporary.[11]

Be careful to look out for all the signposts in your project, including those that help you to know when to pivot. Consistently failing to complete the progress you thought you would make in a given time can be one sign that you are fighting an uphill battle. Another sign is stakeholders not giving you time or support on a project. If people aren't giving you time in their diaries, it may be because the idea is not strong enough to engage your internal clients and therefore your external customers may be even less interested.

Keep up the pace

Most people are motivated by a deadline, and teams are no different. If we have a weekly team meeting on a Tuesday, we tend to leave getting our actions done until the day before. Why do we wait a whole week to complete our actions? Could we instead have a daily meeting and undertake our actions the same afternoon, getting five weeks of progress completed in one week instead?

This is the principle of a sprint, a short period in which a team works intensively to complete a goal[12] and is at the heart of agile working. Many teams work in a sprint because they are responding to an urgent problem, such as an HR and IT team working together to help their teams work remotely when COVID-19 forced people to work from home. Because they are working to a very real deadline or against a huge business need people roll up their sleeves and make it happen.

It is harder to get momentum on a non-urgent project, because when the business is not at risk it feels easier to spread out the work at a comfortable pace, timed by weekly or monthly meetings, with not much progress needed in between. We naturally do this because many of us are working on more than one team and so we are spreading the work out. However, if we don't focus on what needs to be done and get it done as quickly as possible, we risk getting distracted by other projects and our work getting diluted. In today's working environment things change fast, and by the time you deliver your project, it may no longer be relevant. Setting a good, crisp pace for your team's work is essential for creating some momentum towards your goals.

Faster is better. Speed accelerates value creation and intensifies value appreciation. And speed means that more can get done in less time.

Michael Schrage[13]

One of the fastest moving company cultures I've ever worked with is AB InBev. I like to say they work in dog years because they are seven times faster than other companies. When I interviewed Laura Diamond, Head of Consumer Strategy, Insights and Innovation in Europe, she explained to me that the business is very action-orientated, so projects kick-start fast and they test and learn quickly. They focus initially on stress-testing the idea to identify potential risks, making small iterations and improvements, and learning at speed. They are looking for the early signals that tell them to pivot if necessary. Laura tells her teams to 'be calm and unreasonable', keeping an eye on their ultimate goal and accelerating towards it, and making sure they learn as they go.

Even though they work at a fast pace, it is not speed for the sake of it. The balance between rapid progress and reflection is important. The key is to get started quickly, fail early, learn from it and move forward. Rather than speeding ahead blindly, this is working at pace to make progress, then learning and adapting as a result of that progress. Mark Zuckerberg's motto for Facebook is 'move fast and break things', but there is an increasing recognition that moving fast for the sake of speed, without being responsible to customers or society, is no longer considered good practice.[14] Teams need to move with momentum, but allow themselves the time to learn from their work and be responsible to their customers.

Momentum comes from people feeling a sense of ownership on the project, and wanting to progress, rather than reluctantly waiting for actions to be handed out. Think about how you can set a good, fast pace for your team's work that gives immediate, ambitious deadlines, and tightens up your timing to get the job done quicker. There's no need to wait around or stretch it out – achieve your goals earlier, so you can move on as a team to achieving more.

One thing at a time, most important thing first, start now.

Caroline Webb[15]

Tool 14

Accelerate and reflect

If our time expands to fit the available tasks, the risk is that we can spend the whole project journey only just keeping up with our actions and leave no time for reflection. When I worked at ITV Imagine, my boss was Pele Cortizo-Burgess, the Director of Creative Strategy and a legend in the advertising world. Pele was an inspirational leader who gave me many great pieces of advice, such as blaming 'technical issues' is unacceptable (sort them out well in advance), being controversial is far better than being mediocre (be memorable not boring), and have a fluid mindset, using the 'colour and advance' conversation tool. We used this to practise presentations, to help presenters learn to balance between interesting details and the story. When I'm telling a story, and the listeners think I've skipped an interesting bit, they can say 'colour!', which means 'we want more juicy detail before we go further'. If my story is too slow and people are feeling a bit bored, they say 'advance!', which means 'get to the point', or 'tell us what happens next'. If all you do is advance your story, it becomes flat, but if all you do is colour the details, you'll never get to the end.

'Colour and advance' is the inspiration for this tool, which is to find time in your project for moments to accelerate and reflect. Instead of one big long set of actions that the team ticks off, identify the points which you can accelerate and progress quickly and intensely, so that you leave your team time and space in which to reflect, learn and improve the project, before accelerating again.

To use this tool, look at the project journey you have designed, and work out where you can accelerate the work, to provide space for reflection afterwards. For example, if you are a team delivering a conference in four weeks' time, the tasks might look like this.

Week 1	Set the date and time, choose and book the venue, consider who to invite
Week 2	Choose theme, design and send invitations, create content and branding
Week 3	Review RSVPs, set menus, finalise venue set-up and logistics details, send final reminders, create content and printing
Week 4	Rehearse key speeches, set up the venue, deliver the event
Week 5	Pay suppliers, gather attender feedback, wrap up on what went well and what to do differently in future, book the venue for next time – and have a rest

No matter how big or small your event and your team, we tend to work back from the event and spread the tasks out over the four weeks, doing each at the latest possible moment that they are required. We do this because we are avoiding putting too much work in at any one time or for any one person, so we create a gentle pace for the team, with weekly updates on actions. But what if there's no reason to wait? How about if most logistics tasks can be done and out the way in Week 1, leaving your team more time to reflect, adapt and improve the event itself?

This tool asks you to separate 'Accelerate' tasks (actions and progress) from 'Reflect' tasks (learning, improvements, inspiration). Get as many of the Accelerate tasks out the way as early as you can, and put aside some of the time for making the event better.

Here's an example of how a new timeline would look, in the same five-week period, but allowing for the ebb and flow of progress and learning.

Example:
Accelerate and Reflect

Week 1	Accelerate
	Set the date and time
	Choose and book the venue
	Consider who to invite
	Choose theme, design and send preliminary invitations and get initial RSVPs
	Set menus, venue set-up and logistics details

Week 2	**Reflect**
	Review RSVPs, understanding who is coming and why they have accepted and what they want from the event
	Understand who is not coming, why they declined, and if there is anything we can do that might attract them to attend
	Get inspiration from other events people are attending
	Ask attenders who have accepted about the best and worst events they attended in the last year
	Based on RSVPs, inspiration and feedback, create new ideas for making this event more attractive for those who are already coming and to attract those who declined
Week 3	**Accelerate**
	Update the event approach, messaging, agenda, look and feel
	Send fresh invitations to those who declined to see if they will change their minds
	Create content and event branding to reflect the improved event ideas
	Update speakers, logistics and theme if needed
Week 4	**Reflect**
	Reflect on progress and feedback, looking at new and updated RSVPs
	Rehearse key speeches and content and improve them in line with feedback and attendees
Weeks 4 and 5	**Accelerate**
	Finalise all logistics and send out confirmation of agenda to attendees
	Deliver the event
	Pay suppliers and book the venue for next time
Week 5	**Reflect**
	Reflect on feedback, success, and learnings, and create ideas for making the next event even better – and have a rest

Do not mistake activity for achievement.

Mabel Newcomer (1892–1983)

This example demonstrates how you can push as much action and progress as you can into the early stages, leaving the team time to truly reflect and consider. You may worry that this adds to the workload, and it might well do so. At the early stages, this is likely to mean that everyone works in parallel on a number of actions, rather than waiting for one admin person to deliver them sequentially.

By accelerating the work early, you then create the space to reflect, learn and adapt. If you fill the timeline with all actions and no reflection, you can, and will, deliver an average event. Instead of blindly delivering an event without any time to reflect and improve it, you are completing the basic logistics early, to give you time to make your event truly exceptional. Some team members work best when they have time to think and reflect, rather than pushing for action constantly. This helps us to avoid MAFA: mistaking action for achievement.[16]

Make sure you separate your 'Accelerate' meetings from 'Reflect' meetings – it is very hard to evaluate and be inspired at the same time. Even if they need to be on the same day, separate them with a break, or move to a new room to mark a difference between them. Think of this as a lean in, lean out approach – focus on the details, get things done, then sit back and reflect on where you are. Intense actions followed by intense reflection. All of which allow you to improve what your project delivers.

Whether in business or in war, the ability to react quickly and adapt is critical, and it's becoming ever more so as technology and disruptive forces increase the pace of change.

Walter Isaacson[17]

Ready, fire, aim

Perfection is the enemy of progress.

Sir Winston Churchill (1874–1965)

Michael Schrage's book *Serious Play* introduced the concept of 'ready, fire, aim', challenging the more traditional 'ready, aim, fire'. Firing before aiming refers to creating an early version of a new idea (a quick prototype of a new software) to see how people react, and learn from that, rather than working out a list of the perfect requirements before getting started. Michael says the value of prototypes resides less in the prototype itself and more in the interactions that it generates, including the conversations, arguments and consultations that are caused by discussing it.

Eric Ries refers to creating a 'minimum viable product', an early version that allows a team to collect as much learning from customers as they can with the least amount of effort,[18] and the Innovation Leader/KPMG report on innovation shows that successful innovation teams are distinguished by their ability to test, learn and iterate.[19] One innovation client told me that she purposefully gives UX designers challenging deadlines so they don't spend ages crafting and perfecting the look and feel. If it is too polished, she says customers will be reluctant to challenge it and may not get as valuable an insight.

For your team goal, consider what is the earliest possible version of that goal, and how you can experiment with it to get early feedback to learn from. In the Accelerate and reflect example, this was sending out an early invitation to see who would come or not, then use the feedback to improve the event to get more people there. Early ideas are like seedlings – you might see one and not know if it will develop into an oak or a weed – you need to grow it a little first. Most great ideas start with a brilliant need or essence, it's just the execution that needs work. How you work on that execution early enough to get learnings should be your key focus early on. Don't wait until the solution is 100% perfect. Consider launching something early, to get early feedback.

The purpose of an experiment is not to solve the problem, but to generate insights.

Michael Schrage[20]

Tool 15

Measuring success checklist

The final tool is an important one that is often not planned for at the beginning, and can get forgotten at the end, which is measuring whether or not your project has succeeded. We don't tend to plan because we are keen to get started, and figure we will know when we get there. At the end we are moving on to something new and don't have time to measure how we did.

Measuring success is also not simple. Of course, you can tell whether or not you produced an event on a specific date, or you managed to get 90% of the company to benefit from your digital transformation programme. For example, we may have got 90% of the business to benefit from digital transformation, but if the project cost far more than the projected budget, that's not a complete success. If we delivered an amazing event, but with only 50% attendance, it's not a true success, despite us achieving our specific goal. If our wannabe sailor had managed to get to Southampton, but arrived exhausted, sunburned and possibly traumatised after days at sea, would that be a successful outcome? Arguably not.

This is why planning to measure success at the *beginning* of a project, and then actually measuring it at the end is so important. We tend to only measure timing and deliverables, but we also need to measure the outcomes and the journey itself.

Measuring success means working out how the team will know when you have. This checklist gives you some ideas for how you might set up your success targets in three areas: deliverables, outcomes and the journey itself.

Measuring deliverables:

- How will we know we've achieved our specific deliverables?
- How will we know we have delivered on time?
- What will we overhear people saying about our team when we've succeeded?
- How will we know we've delivered within budget?
- How will we know if we've used our resources properly?

Measuring outcomes:

- How will we know we have delivered a quality outcome?
- What are the qualitative signs of success we can use to measure our success?
- What will we tell our families about this project when it is successfully completed?
- What will the company say about our project to its customers if we do a good job?
- What difference will we be able to see outside of our company if we are successful?
- What do we want people to post on social media about this project when we are done?

Measuring the journey:

- How will we know if we've worked well as a team?
- How will we want people in this team to feel at the end of the project?
- What will we have learned on this journey as a team?

> Going through these questions as a team and considering how you will measure your deliverables, your outcomes and the journey itself, you will be able to set up some measures that raise the importance of all three elements of success.

Active recovery

As any athlete will tell you, rest is important, but research has found that switching from high intensity workouts to doing nothing may not be the best way for your body to recover. Which is where active recovery comes in – a low-intensity activity (a walk, a gentle bike ride or a yoga session) on the days following an intense workout that helps muscles to recover and helps them to adapt to the demands placed on them, improving performance overall.

Like in sport, the direction and energy of a team towards a goal is not linear. Bursts of work are followed by periods of reflection on what has been learnt and improvements to be made, for example, by completing a 'Sprint retrospective' between iterations, where a team reflect on what they have achieved so far, and identify improvements to make before the next iteration.[21]

Treat your supercharged team as elite athletes, and plan what you will deliver and when, with natural ebbs and flows of energy for the most effective journey towards your destination.

Key take outs

- A well-developed project plan is the best roadmap to success.
- Pace is important, but don't blindly press on regardless.
- Successful projects maintain a balance of action . . .

- . . . and reflection, because achieving your team goal is not linear.
- Piloting and prototyping saves time in the long run and achieves a better end result.
- Genuine success is measured by not only output and timing, but also outcomes and the quality of the journey itself.

chapter 7

Ways to work together

If you are a team of task-focussed achievers, it's often tempting to just crack on with the work rather than take the time to set up ways of working. But this is a false economy. The highest performing teams work well because they've decided *how* to work together in the best way. Ineffective teams use a standing agenda put together years ago or work in certain ways simply because that's how they have always done it. We are all pressured for time and haven't been able to consider better ways to work because we are only just keeping up with doing our jobs.

When I describe my work as a workshop facilitator to my family, I tell them it boils down to helping adults behave so they can get the best from each other. Poor ways of working together have become the norm, but we don't have to accept them just because that's the way it is. Now we have the chance to change poor practice into truly fantastic teamwork – not only because it's the right thing to do, but because it's the most effective way to achieve our goals.

This chapter gives you simple ways to deliberately decide how to work well together. When your team commits to their own ways of working, they will be able to get the most from each other, and enjoy the work more.

The way a team plays as a whole determines its success. You may have the greatest bunch of individual stars in the world, but if they don't play together, the club won't be worth a dime.

Babe Ruth (1895–1948)

What you will learn in this chapter:

- How to build trust and develop 'teamship' within a team.
- How to agree language, processes and behaviours for a team.
- How to work together effectively when a team works across different locations.

Building trust and teamship

When you think about a great team you have been in, do you think about the work, or do you think about the people you worked with? For me, it's the people.

Thinking back to my first start-up, my team and I led creative workshops for some of the biggest global TV shows in the world. Every year the production teams would meet to share ideas, collaborate and plan, and we made these events happen. Working for the best creatives in the world was inspiring, but not without its challenges.

One project stands out in my memory as the very best of times and the very worst of times for our team. We were working on a very successful TV format with incredibly high-profile clients who were clever and collaborative, but our main contact tended to bully the people around her when under pressure, especially us. As a consequence, we were pushed to deliver far more than had been agreed and budgeted for in a very unpleasant atmosphere. Despite this, our team believed in the project and we worked positively with each other to deliver a brilliant event. I am still proud of that work today, not just for the quality of the workshop we delivered, but for how we were able to work well together, and support each other, despite the difficulties. A decade later, our team from that project remain friends and colleagues, and continue to work together.

Brilliant teams manage to work well together under pressure, so long as they believe in what they are doing and treat each other with respect, especially when things become difficult. For this reason, teams are a great way to make good friends. If you can work well despite the challenges and deliver something excellent together, it feels wonderful long after the project is done.

Teams that respect and value each other are better for us too. Teams that value honest feedback, respect for each other, and openness are 80% more likely to have good emotional wellbeing. Happier employees are up to 20% more productive than unhappy ones.[1]

In order to be efficient and productive, we need to be heard and understood as people. Good teams create a bond with each other, and because of that they can share ideas, concerns and issues openly. Project Aristotle, a research project at Google, investigated the secrets of effective teams. They found that the top two factors for successful teams were 'psychological safety' ("If I make a mistake on our team, it is not held against me") and 'dependability' ("When my teammates say they'll do something, they follow through with it").[2]

Google's intense data collection and number crunching have led it to the same conclusions that good managers have always known. In the best teams, members listen to one another and show sensitivity to feelings and needs.

Charles Duhigg[3]

But team bonding is at risk. Michael Schrage, author, researcher and advisor on the behavioural economics of iterative innovation, says that one of the main things that will change in the future of work is the loss of the water cooler moment: those serendipitous moments between meetings where people connect and catch up.[4] Of course, we can still text, email and talk, but when people work remotely, we have less informal time together because we don't have those moments waiting outside a corridor or grabbing coffee together between meetings. When Michael and I discussed this, he asked me if we should mandate social activities for teams to create a bond.

My answer was that I don't believe we need to make people socialise, we simply need to bring those moments of connection into our meetings more consciously. This can be as easy as asking people about why they are on the project, or what else is happening in their lives, before getting down to work – what we used to do when we weren't so time pressured. The key is that the team gets into the habit of the personal check-in as a regular activity and an important part of the team's business. Michael called this 'efficient socialisation'.

Anne Lewnes, Executive VP and Chief Marketing Officer at Adobe, says that when working remotely, they prioritise talking about people's wellbeing first in remote meetings, asking "How is everybody feeling? What's going on in your group? Do we need to do something to help you?" She says this was even more necessary when teams had to go online rapidly due to the COVID-19 crisis, because people weren't in a great situation at first and needed compassion from each other.[5]

All of this develops teamship, the bond that forms between team members.

Tool 16

Three-point check-in

The three dimensions of working well together as a team are building personal relationships, sharing professional empathy and committing to work together well. These can be organised into three types of questions to ask people at the start of every meeting. Whether you are starting out together or have been working together for years, use this tool to build trust and develop empathy.

How to use this tool:

- At the beginning of a project, or with a new team, get people to answer all three types of question.

- In subsequent meetings, choose one type of check-in sentence per meeting or let people choose which check-in they want to use that day.

- Give people a choice of which specific sentence they want to complete. That way they have some control over what they choose to reveal.

- Always let people know in advance that there will be a check-in to give them some time to think of an appropriate answer. If you spring this type of exercise on people they can feel worried about what to say, which defeats the trust building intent.

Personal check-in:

- Something you may not know about me is . . .
- I am at the stage in life where . . .
- What keeps me awake at night is . . .
- Something else that's going on in my life right now is . . .
- One thing I am thankful for is . . .

Professional check-in:

- The reason I'm on this project is . . .
- You can rely on me in this team to . . .
- I would like this team to help me learn about . . .
- The people I work for want . . .
- The ultimate success on this project for me would be . . .

> **Productivity check-in:**
>
> - The best work I do is when . . .
> - I like to value other people's time by . . .
> - We must make sure that this team does . . .
> - The hardest thing about working in a team is . . .
> - This week my work will be limited by . . .

Setting rules of engagement

To be a good team we need to behave well together. Collective intelligence research[6] has shown that teams who work well let each other speak, taking it in turns to make sure everyone is heard, and they properly listen to what each person says, with empathy. Empathy and balanced airtime are the basis for any solid friendship, and teamship too.

The problem is that good team behaviour doesn't come naturally. In some teams people spend more time pointing out what's wrong with each other's ideas than building on them and suggesting improvements. When we are stressed we are less likely to be able to listen well, empathise with other people, or give each other airtime. At worst, people can become competitive, confrontational and feel they need to battle with each other, rather than work together.

In the marketing industry it is quite common to hear 'warlike' language when people talk about projects. Many teams run wargames, talk about 'battlegrounds', set up 'squads' and 'scrums', and focus on 'key thrusts'. But not every project needs to be a battle, and the language we use can powerfully frame a project and how its team works together.

Head of the Guinness brand at Diageo, Grainne Wafer talked to me about setting rules of engagement. Guinness is one of the world's most iconic brands, and the team works to keep the brand as relevant and popular today as it has been for over 250 years. What struck me most about Grainne's approach was that she set out both the language and the spirit of the work for her team, consciously laying out the rules of engagement, such as:

- We do this work because we love this brand.
- We have been given the time and the freedom to do this well, so let's make the most of it.
- We can hold conflicting views simultaneously.
- We will communicate early and often – WhatsApp/Slack is fine, no need for polished PowerPoint presentations.
- We must challenge each other to make this project authentic to Guinness and worthy of its legacy.
- The impact of this work will be positive for our customers, for the brand and for the people on this team.

Framing the spirit of the work, and therefore how people will work well together, has given positive energy to the project, the team, and their stakeholders.

At the Budweiser Brewing Group, Rachel Green, who trains and leads sales teams in the UK, talked to me about getting people excited and recognising great work, but in simple and easy ways that don't take up too much time. Their sales team has a WhatsApp group where people share team banter, and where people post observations about the market and work questions for quick answers. Rachel says this means that people are constantly connected whether they're sharing something personal or work related.

Whether a new team or a long-standing team who've worked together for years, there is huge value in resetting your rules of engagement together. Things might have changed, new people may have joined, and some processes and behaviours may no longer be needed. Setting up rules of engagement as a team is a crucial step towards supercharging it. So how do you do it?

Tool 17

Our team rules

Using this tool, the team decides on their own rules for how they agree to behave, what they agree to spend time on, and how they agree to communicate. Avoid falling into the trap of using the same rules for every team. The crucial thing here is to make sure that the team consciously and deliberately chooses these rules, and that they are reviewed and updated through the course of the project, especially when new members join.

There are three types of team rules to consider: language, process and behaviours. Use these three-question lists to kick-start your team's discussion, and publish 'Our team rules' to all in the team once you've decided.

Language rules: How do we agree to talk about this project?

The language we use carries meaning, and what you call your team and how you talk about the project can make an enormous difference. Discuss these language questions in your team before you agree your rules:

- Do we have the right name for the project and team? Does our name accurately represent what the team does? What should we be called?

- Are we carrying language baggage, old names or terms that associate us with the past, with other teams or hold us back in some way? How can we change this?

- Can we rebrand our team, our meetings or our work internally so that this team and our stakeholders understand more accurately what we are doing?

- In the language we use, are there terms we need to stop using because they are outdated, incorrect or prejudiced? What language should we use instead?

BCSS
The right language

As a member of the British Cactus and Succulent Society (BCSS) I was asked to lead a group to modernise our branding in order to attract new members. Instead of leading a committee, the very worst example of teamwork I can think of, I agreed to lead an action group for a fixed, six-month time period. The members of the group represented different members and branches, and we were empowered to make decisions and crucially to take action on behalf of the society, not just talk.

Process rules: How do we agree to work together productively?

The way the team works can make decisions and alignment easier. Consider these process questions to lay out your team rules on how to get things done:

- How can we challenge our current agenda to make better use of the meeting time we have?
- How do we make sure that we cover important discussion, debate and decisions in meetings?
- Can we avoid wasting meeting time on items that could be covered as pre-reads, such as meeting minutes, debriefs and updates?
- How often do we need to meet? Can we set the dates in advance and agree that they won't change?
- Do we need to be face to face when we meet, or will video calls do?

- Does everyone need to be at every meeting? Are there sub-teams who could meet more frequently than the whole team?

- Who leads the meetings? Can we rotate the person who acts as the chairperson, and ask different team members to each be responsible for a different meeting to vary the topics, location and meeting style?

BCSS

A good process

In our BCSS action group, we agreed to meet via video conference every month, with the meeting dates and topics for all six meetings set in advance. Each meeting had a pre-read and a prep work task based on the decisions to be taken. Prep work was compiled into one document for the meeting in advance and presented by the host. If people weren't able to attend, they sent in their opinions before each meeting, and we recorded the meetings for them to catch up on the discussion afterwards.

Behaviour rules: What behaviours do we commit to?

Committing to specific behaviours (and agreeing to avoid others) gives a team the best possible chance of success. Ask these questions as a team, and create the rules that suit what you want to achieve together:

- Can we all agree to starting and ending meetings on time, and if people are late we won't wait for them or catch them up?

- Should we all agree to do at least two hours of actions for this project between meetings?

- Could we all agree to complete any pre-read and prep tasks before each meeting?

- How can we best communicate with each other and save each other unnecessary emails? Shall we avoid 'Reply to all' and use an instant messaging group instead of emails where possible?

- How can we challenge each other constructively and respectfully when we don't agree? (if your team is struggling with this, visit Chapter 8)

- What happens when we don't agree, how will we take the final decision?

- Once a decision has been taken, can we all commit to supporting it fully?

BCSS

Constructive behaviour

In our BCSS action group, we agreed early we could only challenge each other's ideas with a better idea – so if we didn't like the idea but had no better alternative, it stayed in place until a better solution was found. We started and ended meetings on time, and most people did their prep work before meetings (or accepted that their opinions weren't included). After six months our action group delivered a full set of new branding guidelines and materials to the BCSS to be used across the group's 70+ branches and 3,000 members.

Tool 18

Distance culture code

Remote working is time-efficient, saves companies money, and can give career and lifestyle benefits to team members. However, it does bring significant challenges to effective teamwork. We can no longer expect that teams will meet face to face regularly, and for some teams they will never be in the same room as each other. Therefore, we need to work on how to best work together despite the distance. In my company I employ around 30 people who work remotely, flexibly and on specific projects. We don't meet very often in person, but we do meet face to face via Zoom, and we have our own culture of working remotely that we ask people to sign up to when they join the company.

If you can't trust your employees to work flexibly, why hire them in the first place?

Adam Henderson[7] Founder of Millennial Mindset

Use the distance culture code to help you set up the best ways of working for your team so that you are making every encounter as productive as possible, building trust and good communication, and reducing the risks of distance getting in the way of teamwork.

Face to face always	Commit to every conversation being face to face, via video conference with cameras on (or using Facetime on your phone if you don't have Zoom or Teams. This helps people to properly connect, build rapport, allows non-verbal communication, and prevents people from multi-tasking while they talk.

3 Ps check-in	Start each meeting with a check-in using the 3 Ps – personal, professional and productivity – tool. As we are not meeting each other socially we need to build our understanding of each other beyond work.
Be honest	Insist on complete transparency so that people can be honest about anything that affects their work, whether personal or related to other work commitments. It is important to communicate early and often, sharing worries early so that we can support each other.
Track time	Track time on different tasks by clocking in and out of timesheets. This makes it easy to see how long tasks take, what time was spent on them, and how much people are working.
Look professional	Even if working from home, people should look professional, dressed as they would be if they were meeting at an office, and don't have a bedroom or personal items in the background.
Buddy up	For junior or new members, arrange for them to work alongside established team members on the first few projects so that they can learn, get feedback and become comfortable in the culture.
In-person time	Schedule regular, in-person working sessions where possible, weekly for teams in the same city, monthly or biannually for those further afield. These can be training sessions or just co-working together in the same room to build relationships.
Rotate meetings	For people working across time zones, we rotate the time of each meeting, so that we respect each other's lives and time zones.

A regular meeting pattern

The final way to work well together as a team is to have regular, scheduled meetings.

Neil Mullarkey has been a member of a successful team longer than anyone else I know. Neil is a founding member of the Comedy Store Players, a team of improv artists who meet and perform every Wednesday live at The Comedy Store London, and have done so since 1985 – 35 years. The members of the group have changed over the years, but there's a core team who have continued to work together, very successfully, for all this time.

Neil says that one of the reasons why the Comedy Store Players have been successful for so long is that they meet in the same place, at the same time, on the same day and they run pretty much the same kind of games every meeting. Because they all choose to be there and they only see each other once a week, they don't get sick of each other like many people who see each other daily. The people in the group do change over time, and new people bring inspiration, but the meeting itself is fixed, predictable and provides the structure around which they all perform at their best.

Back at the Budweiser Brewing Group, the 110 people in the UK sales team have a 15-minute standing team meeting every Tuesday morning. There is a discipline about a regular catch-up, being on time, with everyone there, and the predictability and momentum of knowing there is a meeting to go to.

Make sure meetings are timely, scheduled far enough in advance so that people can plan to be there, and the expectation is that you will attend, or will send your thoughts in advance (rather than expecting the meeting to be rescheduled if people can't make it).

How you work is how you will succeed

Brilliant teams work well together. They don't need to be each other's best friends or socialise often, but they do need to respect each other, be able to challenge each other constructively, and commit to achieving a common goal by making each other's lives easier rather than more difficult. If your team enjoys the work and the people they work with, it will be more successful. Taking the time to consider and agree how you will work best as a team is a crucial step in supercharging your team and will make sure you will do your best work together.

Key take outs

- Connecting on a personal level and building teamship make us happier and more productive.
- Agreeing team rules is crucial to ensuring our team rules.
- Distance is no barrier to effective teamwork.

chapter 8

Dealing with conflict

People who work in high-performance teams challenge each other often, but they do it constructively. Supercharged teams aren't 'nice', they are clever and able to deal with the conflict that is bound to happen, even in the best teams. But when teams work in conflict all the time it is attritional. We must prepare for conflict, as we are likely to disagree over decisions, have personality clashes, and have small misunderstandings. But we must also deal with conflict well and early to keep the positive momentum of our journey towards our goal. The crucial thing to remember is that we need to intervene early to stop things from getting worse over time – or conflict can derail our work and make the team feel terrible, and so negatively impact our work.

What you will learn in this chapter:

- How not to be afraid of conflict.
- How to prepare for and manage conflict early.

- How to address conflict that already exists in the team.
- How to manage individuals who are causing conflict in the team.

Consensus is not our goal

No great team prioritises consensus over conflict. I heard a story about a political party holding a meeting to find consensus on how to merge several Brexit motions, only to find that they couldn't agree on the meaning of the word consensus,[1] and so couldn't go any further. This story epitomises the problem with consensus. When everyone focuses on agreeing with each other and nothing else, the actual work we are there to do is diluted, avoided or becomes impossible.

Being nice to each other for the sake of agreement and to avoid all conflict means that people compromise and make bad decisions without the chance to challenge and improve them. To build strong foundations for our work, we must use constructive conflict to build alignment. Supercharged teams invite constructive conflict, including dealing with any teamwork issues that get in the way.

Conflict and competition can be constructive

In teams, we must challenge each other and hold each other to the highest expectations of performance. Think about being in a sports team. None of us want to be the best person in a bad team but we do want to be a great person in a great team. When you're in a good team you have to raise your own game because of how good the rest of your team are. When you work with great people you can compete with them and challenge them to do better, so that the team itself wins.

One misconception about highly successful cultures is that they are happy, lighthearted places. This is mostly not the case. They are energized and engaged, but at their core their members are oriented less around achieving happiness than around solving hard problems together.

Daniel Coyle[2]

Neil Mullarkey says that improv actors do what they do for the good of the show, so even if people have individual conflicts or don't like each other, they are all focussed on entertaining the audience, which is how they overcome problems and personality clashes. He says that what makes them different is that they're rivals *and* co-creators.

In the book *Collective Genius* the authors[3] refer to 'creative abrasion', a vital part of creativity in which ideas are created, explored and modified through debate. The authors point out that this essential conflict is about the ideas, not each other, and so the conflict becomes intellectual rather than interpersonal.

When alternatives compete in a marketplace of ideas, they get better and the competition often sparks new and better approaches.

Hill et al[4]

The problem is, it is hard not to feel personally attacked if someone challenges one of our beliefs, even if only intellectually. One way to get round this is to use a phrase like this when giving challenging feedback: "I'm giving you these comments because I have very high expectations and I know you can reach them." A team of psychologists found that using that sentence helped people to boost performance and effort even when being given difficult feedback.[5] Kim Scott, author of *Radical Candour*, says we need to "care personally and challenge directly", advising people not to say "You're wrong" but "I think that's wrong".

We need to be conscious of using the right language to constructively challenge each other, so that we can hold each other to the highest standards.

Tool 19

Opinions and instincts

If you avoid conflict at the early stages of a team's work, it could be detrimental to the project later on because you may be postponing important foundational issues that will be more expensive and traumatic to sort out further down the line. This tool helps to flush out disagreement and misalignment at the early stages of a team coming together, giving people permission to express their opinions and instincts and show where they agree or disagree early.

Ask each member of the team to consider these questions carefully, and to answer them individually and without discussion, in writing.

1 If you were the sole decision-maker, what single thing would you do to make us achieve our goal?

2 If we had to make a decision right now on what to do, what would that be?

3 What is the most important challenge we will need to overcome to achieve our goal?

4 What are the traps and time-wasters we need to avoid?

5 What will happen if we do nothing as a team and let nature take its course?

Feel free to reword these questions or create new ones to fit your project, but keep them broad, rather than specific. The questions you use should make people think about the big picture of what you are doing as a team. You are asking people to give personal opinions and share their instincts, and in this way you are more likely to understand their thinking and expose any fundamental misalignment early on.

How to use this tool:

- Send the questions out in advance so people have a chance to consider their answers.

- In a meeting, ask your team to write out their answers, each on a separate Post-it.

- Starting with Question 1, ask people to take turns to read their answer out loud, and then stick it up on a wall. Ask people to stick their answers next to similar ones when they agree, so that themes form around common answers.

- Do this for all the other questions before starting a discussion – so you will have a wall with the answer to all five questions, themed visually in front of you before you start discussing.

- Discuss all the points of agreement first, starting with the biggest themes, and noting where the team are aligned on all five questions

- Then address those areas where you don't all agree, starting with the area that has the least agreement first, and talking each through properly to understand why people disagree. At this point, you are not looking to change people's minds or force agreement, simply to understand the differences and why people feel that way.

- Record a list of areas that need to be covered in future meetings, starting with the most important ones, and address each in turn in subsequent sessions together.

It is important to do this visually, on a wall, (or with pieces of paper on a table if you don't have wall space). If you use the tool verbally, there is a greater risk of people taking the conflict personally. When people disagree while facing each other and looking into each other's eye, the discussion becomes about each other. By looking at the wall together, it is easier to feel the disagreement is about the themes, not the people talking. This tool encourages people to disagree in a structured, neutral way, so that they can move on together, and helps team members to get to know each other early on too.

I've seen this approach lead to two separate teams being formed when it showed that people in the team had completely different projects in mind. I've also seen this tool show where people are making assumptions about language, target consumers or technical know-how, only to find that we were all talking about completely different things. Had we not found these out early, we would have failed to achieve our goals.

Conflict is more common today

Irene Grindell, a professional mediator, is an expert in conflict management with a particular fascination for teams, and when I interviewed her she made the point that conflict is an inevitable part of being in any team. However, Irene has noticed that conflict has become worse at work over the last decade, because people communicate so much through email instead of talking, and so misunderstandings are more frequent, and can escalate quickly.

With the increased pressure we are under at work with more to do, less time to do it in, and reduced attention spans, we have less time to sort out misunderstandings together, or even notice they've happened. To avoid conflict later, Irene's advice for high performing teams is to communicate expectations early on and immediately tackle three things as soon as they arise for the first time: sniping at each other within the team, breakdown in support for each other and vulnerability of one of the team members.

Tool 20

Conflict predictor

Earlier we set our team rules in Tool 17, but every team finds itself under pressure at some point, and with more remote, flexible and gig-style jobs, there are seven common issues that are likely to cause conflict, no matter what team you are in, how good your ways of working are, or how brilliant the people in your team are.

As a team, talk through each of these in turn so you will be able to predict the conflicts that might arise, how to avoid them in the first place, or deal with them when they happen. Working through this list will make some people in the team more aware of the impact they may have on each other, preventing issues from arising.

1 Trust and relationships are hard to build, especially when we are working in different locations. How can we make sure we build relationships both personally and professionally?

2 Personalities clash when people have different expectations of behaviour, like how acceptable it is to be late to a meeting, or how we challenge each other. How will we understand each other's styles and communicate when we feel offended or annoyed?

3 Email can lead to misunderstandings and can make decisions more complicated than they need to be. How can we avoid the wrong tone, being misunderstood or communicating inefficiently?

4 Competing work priorities and workload are hard to manage, and stress can create conflict. How can we plan ahead for busy periods and support busy people?

5 Learning, advice, knowledge-sharing and coaching are harder for managers and team members, so we give each

other less support than we should. How can we make time for learning from each other and giving advice?

6 New team members need 'onboarding', and sharing knowledge adds workload. When people aren't properly briefed, they can cause problems later on. How can we share the load of training new people to get them up to speed?

7 Some team members can be excluded by technology challenges and feel left out, or put under pressure. How can we make sure technology issues don't cause extra worries?

How to use this tool:

- Send these questions out to the team and ask them to read it and consider what's missing. Ask people to add any other areas that may cause conflict, for example, if the previous tool has thrown up severe differences in opinion or instinct, talk through them here to predict where conflict may arise in the project journey, and how to spot it and avoid it early on.

- In a meeting talk through your potential causes of conflict, including any others that people have added, starting with the conflicts that the team feel are most likely and possible for this team.

- For every point, discuss how and when the conflict might happen, how to avoid it or deal with it, and make some commitments to avoid or deal with them.

Many of the most common symptoms of conflict – assuming the worst of each other, making assumptions about each other's intentions, dealing with different agendas, priorities or disagreements, competing for resources, and not understanding each other's perspectives or communication styles – can be avoided if you use Tools 19 and 20.

What to do when a team is already in conflict

If you are in a team that is already in an established pattern of conflict, my heart goes out to you. Being in a team in conflict can be soul-destroying, especially when the conflict is day in and day out in a long-standing team with no end in sight. If we spend a lot of our lives at work, and that work consists of being part of a team, and that team is not functional, it can be attritional.

Irene is brought in to mediate work conflicts when toxic situations have gone too far. In her experience, being in a team that is full of conflict can be one of the most traumatic life experiences a person can face. She explained that when a team conflict becomes traumatic, it can lead to people missing work, which then has a knock-on effect for the team and often makes the conflict worse. For the individual at home they have plenty of time to ruminate, which makes returning to the workplace difficult. Whilst back in the workplace, people have started to pick a side and the whole team can end up entering the 'conflict zone'. When people have been avoiding confronting the conflict, the fear of facing it becomes overwhelming and the relationship becomes even more stressful. Irene's main advice is to have a conversation as early as possible about a team conflict and immediately talk about the impact that the conflict is having on the individuals before it escalates.

The negative effects of unchecked conflict can be enormous, resulting in long-term sick leave, grievances, absenteeism and even legal action. The commercial cost alone is huge – poor mental health costs employers up to £45 billion a year in Britain, and employers are increasingly embracing staff wellbeing for this reason.[6] Sorting out conflict at work is not only the right thing to do for the mental health of employees, but also for the commercial benefits to the business.

Conflict resolution is about listening to each other, shifting our understanding and moving on together. The next tool helps the team deal with existing conflict before it goes too far.

Tool 21

Six reasons why

This is a simple tool I've used many times with different teams to address situations that went badly, understand why they happened, and learn from them for the future.

- Ask each individual team member to think of something this team worked on in the last year that went well or felt good, and list three reasons why it went well.

- Ask each individual team member to think of something that did not go as well as hoped in the last year, or did not feel good. List three reasons why.

- Send these questions to people in advance so they can think about which situations they want to share.

- Ask people to make the reasons descriptive, so instead of writing just one word such as, 'time' write 'we had enough time to prepare well'.

- When you come together as a team, ask each person to write down their reasons on separate Post-its, so each person has in front of them six Post-its: three with reasons why something went well, and three with reasons why it did not.

- Ask people in turn to share their positive examples first. They should mention the project briefly, but spend the time on the three reasons why it went well, sticking their three examples up on a wall or flipchart, before the next person shares their three positive examples.

- Theme similar thoughts together, so if several people mention having enough time to prepare (even if referring to different projects), put those together.

- When you've got all the three reasons why things went well and themed them, you will see why things go well, usually to do with communicating early, having time to prepare, having the right people on the team, and so on. Make sure you identify the key themes as a group before moving to the projects that went badly.

- Then repeat the exercise for the projects that went badly. Ask people in turn to briefly describe their project, and the three reasons why, putting them up on the wall and building common themes. Often you will find that the reasons why things go badly are the exact opposite of the reasons why things go well, such as not enough time, being brought in at the last minute, no clear briefing, or the wrong people on the team.

- Once you have the themes for the projects that went badly, focus the discussion on the reasons why, not the projects themselves, talking through why things go badly and how to avoid those issues in future.

This tool is simple, but it really works. One team had a boss who was never on time, cancelled meetings at the last minute and didn't answer any emails, so the team couldn't get decisions from him and make progress on their work. We brought together the boss, his five direct reports and his PA and through this tool every person, including the boss and the PA shared their six reasons why.

We established that successful projects happened when his team were able to talk with him, even briefly, to get his opinion, and that projects went badly when he cancelled meetings that they were relying on having. After the exercise, he agreed not to cancel meetings, so even if he could only offer ten minutes rather than the full hour booked, they would go ahead (and his PA helped to make this change happen).

It works well because people focus on what's right before what's wrong, so there is a constructive set-up. It allows people to have a bit of a moan about what has gone badly, but in a structured way that highlights the causes rather than the situation itself. And like previous tools, it focuses the team on a set of themes on a wall rather than directly and challenging each.

However, this tool does assume that the conflict has not gone too far and is still possible to fix as a team. If you are in a team already at war with each other, with historic issues and a lot of baggage, you will need to bring in a conflict mediator like Irene.

Useful critics and brilliant jerks

What about if the conflict in a team is caused by one individual? Now that's really tough. Just like conflict can be good for collaboration, difficult people can play an important role in a team. I like to look for a 'useful critic' in any new project, because I know that that person will bring up issues that others might not mention, or issues we may avoid, to our cost. I know that if we win the critic over, we can really succeed.

Richard Watkins, an expert in team dynamics and collaboration, says that a difficult individual is often a gift. In his work he likes to think of the group as one system, where each person plays a part in the whole. Often a decent proportion of people avoid bringing any conflict or problems to the surface, so a difficult teammate can be seen as a kind of early warning signal. What at first glance looks like one person's drama might be a sign of something bubbling beneath the surface that needs to be addressed. So instead of jumping to blame it could be a good time to understand what that person brings that is useful.

How do you know if someone is a useful critic or just a brilliant jerk? Brilliant jerks are people who do such great work that the team or company accept their bad behaviour because of the benefits they bring. I once worked in a company where a well-known manager had formal complaints of bullying made against him, with several people in his team being signed off work with depression and stress. He went through an official disciplinary procedure and was about to be managed out of the business, when he won a multi-million-pound client deal and the claims disappeared, and he carried on. Not every company is like that, and companies like Netflix have a policy of not hiring brilliant jerks. CEO Reed Hastings says, "Some companies tolerate them. For us, the cost to effective teamwork is too high."[7]

I asked Irene what to do about difficult individuals. She says that a person who is seen as an 'attacker' or bully in a team often has not realised that their way of behaving affects others. Because other people don't always say anything, they are oblivious to the impact that they're having. Irene says you also need to work with anyone who feels attacked to understand their role as well. Often by saying nothing or not communicating, they haven't let others know how they are affected by their behaviour.

Her advice to anyone facing conflict is to deal with it early and immediately, feed back on how a person makes you feel and say something, rather than nothing. The worst thing you can do is not say anything and hope that it will change and improve, because it inevitably will become more serious without intervention.

Irene believes that most people just want to get along and do the work, but some people have a tragic way of getting their needs met so her advice is to challenge the behaviours not the person.

Tool 22

Individual intervention

Use this tool when there is someone causing tension and conflict in the team. Let's call them Person X instead of 'the difficult person' or 'the aggressor' so we don't prejudge them.

Use this tool early on, even on seemingly small issues, as you don't need to wait until things get really bad. If you have an HR person who can support you, get them involved from the start, preferably as soon as you have an inkling there is an issue.

---

1 **Identify the specific change you want**

- Before the intervention, agree what change you want to make happen. Do you need Person X to stop doing their emails during team meetings? Be very specific about the change you need and what that specifically looks like before you do anything.

- Everything you prepare should be focussed on making that one change happen, rather than a shopping list of changes.

2 **Consider the conversation setting**

- Who is the best person in the team to have the conversation with Person X? It's not best done as a whole team, or they may feel under attack.

- Where and when should the conversation take place? Should it be in person, on a particular day of the week, in a neutral setting, or walking round a park rather than facing each other across a table?

3 **Script an intervention statement**

- Write a script beforehand with key bullet points you want to make.

- Start with a top-line reason for the meeting – a brief description of what you want to share and get.

- Talk first about the positive contribution the person makes to the team, what they do well, when they are at their best.

- Then talk about what the team is finding difficult, focusing on one or two specific examples only, with how these examples make people feel. For example, instead of saying 'We think it's really rude to be doing your emails instead of focussing on our team meetings', say 'When you are on emails during our team meetings, it makes us feel like you don't see us or the meeting as important.'

- Then end with a positive wish to move forward to make a positive change, for example, 'I really hope we can work out how to get your full attention in our team meetings and make sure the whole team feels you value their time too.'

4 Question, listen, understand

- Once the intervention has been made, wait and listen to what Person X has to say. Try not to leap in with excuses or conversation fillers, but listen and empathise with how they are feeling at that point.

- They may be defensive or try to explain their behaviour, and the best way to engage with them is to keep asking questions rather than fight back with facts. Ask questions like "You seem to be surprised about this feedback, so has it come as a big surprise?" or "I understand you disagree with this feedback, so how do you see the situation differently?"

- Keep questioning, listening and understanding and play back to them what they are saying so they feel heard, for example, "So the reason why you are on emails is because you are very stressed and you would rather attend and multi-task rather than not attend at all."

5 Moving forward

- Make sure that Person X feels like you really understand them, and only then gently shift to moving forward.

- You can do this by saying something like "Coming back to the team feeling as if you are not valuing their time in meetings, what changes can we make to improve the situation and make the team feel you do value their time?"

- Keep coming back to the impact they are having on the team and how they can make that impact more positive. You may need to do this several times to remind Person X about how they make other people feel.

6 Record commitments

- Write down what you and Person X agree to do to improve the situation, and make these as specific as possible, preferably in Person X's own words, for example, "Even though I'm very busy, I will not be on emails in team meetings and will focus on the meeting so that I value people's time – and if I need to do emails I'll miss the team meeting rather than multi-task."
- Agree to review these commitments after a few weeks.

Dealing with bullies

No matter how much you intervene, some people will not accept responsibility for their actions or consider the impact on other people. Irene calls these 'true bullies'. Although she hates the label and recognises that it is emotionally loaded, sometimes there is such a high-conflict person that little can be done to help them adjust their behaviour.

If you want to supercharge any team, you must prevent bad behaviour so that people can work well together. Aggression at work can lower psychological wellbeing and life satisfaction, lower levels of self-esteem, and cause higher absenteeism, health problems and burnout.[8] Dealing with bullies is absolutely crucial to team and organisational success. If there is a member of your team who is a true bully, remove them from your team – or the cost will be far higher than the benefit.

Confronting a bullying client

As anyone who works in an agency will tell you, being bullied by a client can be very difficult, as they are in a position of power, and their behaviour is not in your control. Recently my team worked for a client who, inexplicably to us, was putting most of her effort into discrediting our work. We had the best team on the job, but no matter who she worked with, she attacked all of us. Trying to resolve our issues directly with her didn't work and we all began to dread the project. It affected our team's mental health – never a great way to get the best work out of people!

We finally found a solution. We agreed as a team that we would never, ever talk to her without a witness from her organisation present. This meant not answering the phone if she called and always insisting on having her other team members in any meeting, going as far as cancelling meetings unless another client attended. After that, her unreasonable behaviour was witnessed time and again by the people in her own team, and she was eventually managed out of the client business.

Whatever you do, don't ignore it

Badly behaved teams and dysfunctional ways of working are incredibly traumatic, and conflict needs to be dealt with. It is very stressful to belong to a team facing constant conflict, and the work the team does suffers. If you ignore conflict and hope it will go away it is likely to get worse, rather than better. Make sure you intervene as a team, so that you can move forward in constructive ways.

Great teamwork is important for job satisfaction and is good for business. Supercharged teams work together constructively to solve problems and make good decisions, without fighting. So, to keep your team happy to make your work successful, and deal with conflict, don't ignore it.

Key take outs

- -

- Conflict can be beneficial and constructive – agreeing with each other for the sake of avoiding conflict is not healthy for the team.
- Planning for conflict and how you will manage it is crucial for swift, effective resolution.
- You can only resolve existing conflict by going through what's causing it – there is no magic button to press and reset.
- Early intervention with individuals causing conflict in the team is paramount.

chapter 9

Get support from leaders

Supercharged teams get support from their leaders. A leader sits outside your team with a level of power and decision-making that will influence your team and its work (rather than a 'team leader' who sits in your team). Most teams have leaders who influence our work, whether they are responsible for funding our project, approving key decisions or giving valuable advice. If your team's work is not sponsored by the important and influential decision-makers in your organisation, the efforts of your team may be wasted. In busy teams we can forget to seek this support, or assume our leader agrees, or worst of all, wait for permission from them for decisions.

Supercharged teams hold leaders to account and take responsibility for getting them to support our work. Leaders are different from stakeholders – they are the bosses, the people who have given your team the sanction to do the work and who then represent you to a more senior group of people. They may also be people that you ask for resources or permission.

These tools help you get the sponsorship and support you need from the leaders to ensure successful outcomes for your team.

What you will learn in this chapter:

- How to effectively 'manage up' to influence your leaders.
- How to get a clear direction of travel from your leaders.
- How to motivate your leaders to help and support your team.
- How to connect your leaders with your customers.
- How to support your leaders to give you perspective.

Why managing up is so important

'Managing up' means influencing our bosses and leaders, and 'managing down' refers to managing a team of direct reports. In my experience, managing up is most often a term used with derision: "She's good at managing up" implies she expends more effort looking good in front of the bosses than making sure her team is ok. The implication is that people who are good at managing up are sycophants. However, managing up is not sucking up.

Being good at managing up is crucial to the success of any team. It helps you to achieve your goals, it's better for business, makes your project easier earlier, and helps your team members develop their careers too.

Head of Innovation, Claire Emes leads strategic projects at Ipsos, a global research agency, and has many years of experience of managing both teams and leaders. I asked her what advice she could give me in managing up. Claire told me she involves her leaders at the very early stages of developing a new strategy by having lots of small conversations over the course of the work, rather than presenting in a big 'ta-da!' moment at the end. She also said she invites leaders to participate in any events where the strategy is shared with wider teams. By involving leaders in the original thinking *and* in the alignment with their teams, they are able to support the delivery of the strategy at all levels.

In a survey of people working in big businesses like Google, Cisco, Bose, ESPN and Capital One, getting support from leaders was identified as a crucial enabler of success in innovation projects.[1] A huge McKinsey study analysed the careers of tens of thousands of managers and found that managing upward and managing horizontally (managing peers and stakeholders) is good for business, good for your career, and is arguably 50% more important in terms of impact than how you manage your subordinates.[2] We will cover how to manage horizontally and successfully engage stakeholders in the next chapter. This chapter gives you some of the main approaches for successfully managing upwards, because while getting support from your leaders is essential to making progress as a team it is challenging.

Collaborative command

In the past, working culture was more 'command and control', where bosses had authority over subordinates who did what they were told.[3] This formal, military-like hierarchy was due to greater market predictability and a steadier pace of work relying on central decision-making, and works particularly well in traditional countries and cultures.

However, recently companies have had to deal with market disruption and a rapid pace of change in order to be able to move fast and flex when needed, becoming more like organisms than machines.[4] NASDAQ refers to this as 'collaborative command', when teams own key decisions,[5] and we take responsibility for goals individually and collectively rather than relying on those in charge to decide everything for us.[6]

However, this means our teams don't always have clear advice from those in charge. Depending on the type of leader you have, it can feel like we have to second-guess or mind-read what our leaders may want.

I've seen this happen more often in the last five years, especially when the team is moving fast, when people are busy, and when the business is good at pivoting. It can become difficult for the team to know if we are going in the direction that our leader would agree with, or if indeed that direction has changed without us knowing.

I'm afraid it's too easy for us to say 'our leadership doesn't support, understand, listen to or communicate properly with' our team, even if this is true. Supercharged teams share the responsibility of getting the support they need from leaders, with their leaders. It is up to our team to make sure we are getting our bosses to collaborate with us to agree on the right direction together, and check in on that direction.

Creating a clear expected direction with your bosses (even if the decisions are ultimately yours) is essential, and your team cannot progress without it.

Netflix

Context, not control

Netflix calls this 'context, not control'. It wants every team to have the insight and understanding it needs to make good decisions by working within the context (business strategy, metrics and measurement, and understanding how decisions will be made) and avoiding control (top-down decision-making, management approval, committees and processes that become more important than the results). You can see why I'm such a fan – as you know I believe we should avoid the time-wasting, energy vacuum that is a committee.

They also talk about teams being 'highly aligned and loosely coupled', where the strategy and goals are clear, with teams focusing on strategy and goals rather than tactics, trusting each other without having to approve each other's work, so they can move fast. Leaders become coaches rather than dictators, and their job is to get the best from their teams.[7]

Relentless prioritisation

We must realize – and act on the realization – that if we try to focus on everything, we focus on nothing.

John Doerr[8]

The origin of the word 'priority' is from the Old French 'priorité' meaning precedence, from the Latin 'prior' meaning 'first'[9] So, as Manoush Zomorodi points out in her book *Bored and Brilliant*, there are no 'priorities', and a priority can only be one thing, but not more than one, if we take the original meaning. In any team it is easy to take on several priorities, but if you want to be truly effective it is about deciding clearly where you will focus, as well as where you will not.

Priorities are good for people too. We can't concentrate on more than a few things at once. Research has shown that younger team members in particular benefit from clearly set expectations and goals, and one-third of employees say 'unclear expectations from supervisors' are their number one stressor in the workplace.[10]

The highest performing companies I work with have a priority-driven culture, and every single activity they do at work is linked to the ultimate achievement of their three key priorities for that year, measured by specific targets. Their targets ladder up to match and deliver their leader's targets, and the boss of their leader's targets after that. Understanding your boss' priority is important, as it will be based on what is good for the business and what is good for them.

North Star metric
A clear direction

Many agile businesses are establishing a North Star metric, a term coined in Silicon Valley that helps businesses to 'move past generating short-lived growth and focus on creating retainable long-term customer growth and a sustainable future'.[11] This is a key measure of success for the product team in a company, linking what the team is working to provide for customers with the revenue the business will generate by doing so.[12]

Examples of North Star metrics include:

- **Airbnb:** Nights booked
- **Facebook:** Daily active users
- **WhatsApp:** Number of messages a user sends

Notice that the examples are not specific destinations (containing dates or financial targets), but they are clear directions instead. This is because as markets and customers are constantly changing, and companies must keep evolving, even their goal needs to stay agile.[13]

A clear direction can help many different companies work together for a common goal. WPP is a global marketing and advertising business, with a huge portfolio of agencies in 225 countries. Despite the scale, it manages to make sure that consumers see consistent and integrated communications on big brands like Colgate Palmolive across the world. To do this, it set up an agency consultancy called WPP: Red Fuse to bring together all the best ideas for this one client, establishing a clear direction for the work, no matter which agency or market you work in. CEO Carl Hartman told me, "We can get the best talent from across WPP to work together brilliantly on Colgate Palmolive because we have a common goal and operating system, and our work is ultimately higher quality, faster and more impactful for our client as a result."

Whether or not you define a North Star as a true metric, or simply a means of establishing a clear direction, knowing what the business is ultimately aiming to achieve, no matter what the project, is important. Your team will already have their specific destination, goals and measures of success, but how that fits into the direction of the company is important to understand. Agreeing a direction rather than a specific destination with your leader means that your team can adapt and flex, while being sure they are travelling with the right intention.

In my consultancy, we ask our individual clients how each project will help them to achieve their targets for the year, and where possible we take the exact wording of their target and use it as a measure to keep the project on track. If a team knows what the leader's targets are, we can understand how our work can contribute towards them achieving their goals.

Tool 23

Direction of travel

If you want to build a ship, don't drum up men to gather the wood, divide work and give orders. Teach them to yearn for the vast, endless sea.

Antoine de Saint-Exupéry[14]

It would be great if we could simply ask our leaders to tell us their targets, the North Star, and how to know if our team is going in the right direction. With some of the best leaders, you can ask those questions and they will tell you, because they know the answer, and are happy to share it.

However, I've come across many an evader-of-direct-questions in my career. Many of us will have worked with leaders who are hard to pin down (don't want to commit to one direction), slippery (don't know the answer so avoid answering it), flip-flop (want to be allowed to change their minds), political (don't have a clear answer because it is based on what other people think), or their hands are tied (it's not up to them but they don't want to admit it).

These leaders don't want to be held accountable in case they are found to be wrong later on. I have a lot of sympathy for

---

them. Some businesses are brutal places to work, and it can be a legitimate survival strategy to go with the flow rather than stand for something that you may be judged further on down the line. If, for example, your leader knows that there is a big restructure on the horizon, they may not be able to tell you, but want to avoid giving you the wrong information until the big announcement comes.

Conversely, you may have a micromanaging leader who wants to be a part of all your decisions and is a bottleneck to progress, thinks they know exactly the route your team should take, or is so specific you may as well hand over all the decisions to them, and not explore any other options. Managing your leaders is tough, I know. However, that doesn't stop us from fixing a direction of travel together with our leader, even if it has to change. A direction of travel should feel possible for all teams and leaders to agree. It is not so specific that a leader feels pinned down, but is a guiding light for the team to work with.

This tool is about asking your leader what they really, really want, so you have a clear direction of travel to work within as your project progresses. There are three sets of questions to ask them: how this team fits into the business strategy; how this team's work affects their personal targets; and what that means for the direction this team takes.

Business strategy:

- How does this team's work fit into the organisation's strategy?
- What is the business North Star, and where does our team fit into that?
- What value will this team bring to the organisation?
- What value will this team bring to our customers?
- What game are we in, as a business (for example, attention, transaction or productivity)?[15]
- What effect will this team have on the business when our project is successful?

Leader's targets:

- What are your targets, and how does this project fit with those?

- How does this team's work help you meet your goals and targets?

- What does a successful project look like to you (deliverables, objectives)?

- What are you most excited about this team achieving?

- How can this project make you look good?

- Beyond the day to day, what concerns you about this project, your work, the business?

- What is your long-term ambition for your career, team or department?

Direction for this team:

- What is the one direction this team should focus on?

- What should we never lose sight of?

- What is your long-term wish or goal for our team?

- What does a successful outcome look like for this team?

- What will you hold us accountable for?

- What may we hold you accountable for?

- What might cause us to change direction?

- How long shall we stay fixed in this direction?

How to use this tool:

- Choose the three most appropriate questions to ask your leader from each section (up to a maximum of nine questions in total). Base your choice on the project and the questions you think your boss would want to answer. I would always suggest asking a few questions per section, rather than just one. A choice of questions means they are not forced to answer something they don't know how to.

- Send your questions to your leader(s) in advance, explaining that the team would like to set a direction of travel in order to get their support for the project.

- Explain that these questions are discussion starting points only, and they don't need to fully commit or answer them perfectly, and ask them to come to the next team meeting ready to discuss their thoughts.

- Invite your leader to your team meeting, and begin the meeting with a short description of your project, outcomes, objectives and timeline to update them, and then ask them the direction of travel questions.

- Ask each question in turn, or ask them to answer the questions they felt most useful first. Make sure all the team are listening, questioning and taking notes, summarising the key points.

- After the meeting, create a summary as a team of the one or two main points they made under each heading, and be sure to repeat the language and wording they used where possible.

- Follow up by sending your leader a direction of travel summary that puts in writing the key points they've made, showing how your team will work towards those (inviting comments and edits). Let them know that your team will work in this direction of travel, and invite them to update it or discuss it through the course of the project.

- Every time you see your leader again, whether in the corridor, at the next company-wide meeting, or in your next team update, make sure you're checking in on the direction of travel, and understand if anything has changed.

If you have more than one leader, you can choose to run the above tool together with all the leaders in the room at the same time, or in separate meetings. If you have all the leaders in the room at the same time, make sure you ask them all to answer the questions in this order: the business strategy questions first, then the personal target questions, and finally the direction of travel questions. Leaders may not want to reveal personal targets in front of each other, so consider doing this one individually afterwards. Agreeing a direction of travel with your leaders will help your team to stay on track and be supported throughout the life of your project.

What's in it for them?

The most basic of all human needs is the need to understand and be understood. The best way to understand people is to listen to them.

Ralph G. Nichols

Over the last year I have had the privilege to work with Stefan Homeister, a leadership expert who has worked with leaders like Steve Jobs, Unilever's Paul Polman and P&G's David Taylor[16] When Stefan and I first discussed great teamwork, he told me that the best teams hold themselves and everybody else accountable, including our leaders. Stefan told me that you may not have a choice of who is your leader, but you can and must choose to influence them, advising teams to "start from your leader's needs, not your frustration with them", no matter whether you work in a small or large organisation, no matter whether you are an intern or the CEO.

Stefan believes that leaders are there to help teams by clarifying success, enabling progress and removing roadblocks. His advice for getting leaders to do this well is to understand why your leaders do what they do, and what they expect from the team, and only then asking for that support. It is only through this understanding that a team can change or challenge, and therefore help improve, what their leader does. Stefan believes modern leaders are not only open to this, they even expect and demand it.

Your leader has to be motivated to help and support your team, which means we should consider what's in it for them. In his book *High Output Management*, Andrew Grove points out, "When a person is not doing his job, there can only be two reasons for it. The person either can't do it or won't do it; he is either not capable, or not motivated."[17] Let's assume for now that your leader is capable of supporting your team, so what will motivate them to do so?

We need to understand our leaders better and look for their motivations. When you work in sales, you get to know your clients as well as possible. Many salespeople I know write down everything they find out about their clients, including the names of their children, their hobbies and their favourite football team. While this may seem creepy, it is a way to make sure you talk to people about what's important to them, deepening the relationship and the trust between you.

Looking back on successful projects I've been a part of, every project gave a unique motivation to the leader that supported it. I can think of five types of motivations that made the leader want to support the project:

- **Success-makers:** The leader could see this project would help them to achieve their performance or profit targets when we created a new range of natural shampoos in Brazil that tested well early on, and eventually led the haircare market for years.

- **Profile-raisers:** The leader looked good in front of their bosses, industry peers and potential future employers when our project approach was innovative enough to win industry awards.

- **Currency-creators:** The project gave the leader something new, interesting, funny or clever to talk about, for example, when we worked to create the mobile phone of the future, or to improve sexual satisfaction through devices, or to empower women to buy themselves a diamond ring rather than waiting to be proposed to. Whether you'd bring them up at a dinner party is debatable, but they were fascinating to work on.

- **Capability-boosters:** Projects where the leader learned something new at first hand, like Unilever CEO Paul Polman who made a habit of visiting the homes of consumers and the stores of customers in every country he visited at Unilever, and so understood people not just from PowerPoint presentations but through rich, memorable experiences.[18]

- **Purpose-generators:** When a leader feels the project is doing something for the greater good on a topic they are passionate about, such as sponsoring a project to reduce packaging and increase sustainability in consumer goods or improving gender equality in advertising.

Finding out what motivates your boss is particularly important when you get a new one. Sue Phillips, Global Head of Insight at Ipsos, told me that when Ipsos combined with Synovate, she found herself reporting to a boss she hardly knew, who had little expertise in qualitative research, her speciality. Sue decided to travel from London to Brussels to meet with her new boss, both to understand more about him and to show him her plans for the year. Sue invited herself – she hadn't waited to be invited. Despite knowing very little about each other, they found common ground and understood each other, which gave her work a solid foundation of support. Always take time to listen and understand the leaders who will influence your project, and you will know better how to motivate them to support you more.

> **Above all, a leader must be trusted and respected. Trust between a leader and constituents opens up two-way communication, making it possible for them to realize their common goals.**
>
> **Marvin Bower**

Tool 24

Leader listening tool

Really listen to your leader. What do they talk about, what do they get excited about, what makes them angry, and what stories do they like to tell? Look for true connections and understanding between you. What, if anything, do you agree on, do you have in common, and what is your common ground together? Listening will help you to identify what might motivate them to support your project.

This tool is based on the five leader motivations and will help you to think through what might motivate your boss. This can be done during any meeting, or with any email contact you have, and it can also be done by 'social media listening' if they are on social media, having a look at what they like, post, share and comment on.

The first step in this tool is to listen and take notes. Think of yourself as a journalist or a qualitative researcher. Write down the exact language your boss is using, word for word, in as much detail as you can. As you listen, you are listening for these clues:

Success-makers: What does success look like to them?

- Do they describe performance, targets, winning, competing and the end results when they talk about success?

- What are the successes they post, write, like or share on social media?

- What are the specific words you can use when you next talk to them about the objectives, deliverables and outcomes of the project?

Profile-raisers: How do they like to be seen?

- Do they talk about impressing anyone, bringing someone on side, or looking good in front of another group?

- Do they worry about, warn you about or want to look better in front of someone?
- Who do they follow, admire, like or repost on social media?
- Do they talk about achieving something specific in the next role or the next few years?

Currency-creators: What would they like to say about this project?

- What stories do they tell you, what do they laugh about, what are they most interested in when they ask about the project?
- Which case studies, examples or topics do they mention regularly?
- What type of things do they talk about when you see them at the coffee machine?

Capability-boosters: What do they want to learn from this project?

- What qualifications do they have on their signature, LinkedIn profile or CV?
- Do they mention any courses, training or leadership programmes?
- Do they talk about learning, lessons, applying learning or learning from mistakes?

Purpose-generators: How does this project fit with their values?

- What do they say they care about? What causes do they support? What charities do they donate to?
- What are their hobbies? What do their hobbies say about them? What do they *want* their hobbies to say about them?
- What are they passionate about, known for or have been involved in?

How to use this tool:

- One way to use this tool is to ask them the questions next to each motivator and write down what they say – if they are the sort of leader who will be comfortable being questioned in that way.

- Sometimes it's easier and more comfortable to listen, take notes and analyse their motivations afterwards rather than questioning them. You may not want them to know you are analysing what motivates them. In this case, you can use the notes you took in the direction of travel tool, other meeting notes, what you find on social media, and any other presentations you hear them give.

- When you have your notes, take the key topics, words and phrases your leader has used, and plot them where they fit along the five different types of motivation.

- Do this as a team by putting up a flipchart on a wall for each of the five motivators, and getting people to write down key phrases, language and topics from their notes on Post-its, and put them up on the relevant flipchart. An alternative would be to create a shared Google doc for the team (structured in the five motivators) in which team members can record observations from individual meetings to share with the full team, keeping this populated on an ongoing basis.

- Share and discuss the language, topics and phrases you have recorded for each motivator. You should be able to tell where your leader is motivated by what they have talked about.

- It is rare for people to be motivated in just one area, so you may find you have a better idea of how to motivate them to support your project in several different ways.

- Keep these motivations, and the specific language or topics in mind, to use them in the next update or the next time you talk. So, if your boss talks about "a shift from efficiency to quality", bring that phrase up in the next meeting. If your boss talks about a big conference coming up, remember to ask them about it, and whether this project could be the topic of a new presentation next year. If they like to use sports analogies, create a story for the project around an analogy of being an elite sports team and the coaching you need from them.

Paraffin

Let leaders talk first

In my business we aim to make our clients' lives easier and make their projects a success internally. An important part of delivering that is a clear understanding of how our work fits into the rest of their job. However, as a consultancy, we often only see the one project, not the many others they are working on and pressures they face. When we have tight timelines and only a quick meeting to catch up in, it is all too tempting to jump on a call and leap straight into project updates, questions and actions.

However, in every single conversation, I ask how they are and whether anything has changed since we last saw them. You may have 30 minutes booked, and spend 20 minutes listening to them, but those 20 minutes will be far more valuable to the project than spending all the time on your updates. You will know what they are worried about, and you will have a wider context about your work and their concerns, so your updates will be more relevant. Always start every conversation with a client or a leader by letting them talk first, no matter how tight you are for time.

In communication, speaking is important, but listening is probably even more important. It's the quality of your listening that will shape the other person's speaking. Not everything must be said.

Esther Perel[19]

Involve them directly

In our interactions with our leaders, it is our job to make sure we build their understanding of our team, our project, our customers or the issue we are working on. One of the best ways to do this is by giving them direct contact with the customer, issue or topic, so they experience it at first hand. All too easily today we can Google something, listen to a presentation about something, or see something on social media which makes it feel like we don't need to experience it ourselves.

I remember in the early days of mobile phones, when you had to limit how many texts and calls you made because they were so ridiculously expensive. However, all our mobile phone clients, no matter how junior, had unlimited calls and data, which meant there was no way they'd understand how their customers had to count the texts or avoid talking to someone because of cost. When I work with scientists who make toothpastes, they often start from an assumption that people brush their teeth twice a day. Imagine their horror when I sat them down in a 10am workshop with a young man who explained to them why he felt brushing your teeth in the morning was a waste of time. It is very important that decision-makers have direct access to the real context of the project, topic or customer.

Sometimes the best way to get leaders to support you is to put them directly on the front line. Unilever was one of the very first big companies to ask every senior manager, all the way to board members, to visit their consumers at home on a regular basis. At Pret a Manger, every new employee, no matter how senior, works for one week on the shop floor when they first join the company and spends two days a year in the shop thereafter. We do this in our public sector work too. Recently on a project asking communities to come up with ideas for reducing crime in their area, we didn't just send out a survey. Instead, the local councillor who would make the decision on funding joined existing community meetings around the city, met with residents and heard their concerns and ideas at first hand.

The fundamental difference in professional intervention is no longer about transmission of expertise – it is about the cultivation, transformation and building of the capabilities of your client.

Michael Schrage[20]

Keeping your leaders grounded in customer needs can help with creating 'servant leadership', a term coined by Robert K Greenleaf[21] to help leaders remember the needs of constituents rather than on his or her own performance or image.[22]

Unilever
Connecting with consumers

Paul Polman talks about staying humble as a leader. He says many people around you tell you how great you are, and you can find yourself living in a bubble, forgetting how privileged you are.[23] For this reason, Unilever's CMI team still encourages every employee, from factory workers all the way up to the CEO, to meet customers and consumers. One of the ways they do this is through an 'always-on' online platform where employees can have virtual meetings with consumers anywhere in the world. They can request a meeting with a soup lover from Kenya next week at 4pm and will automatically receive a meeting invite to a live video chat. They then record their observations to share any insights with the rest of their team on an in-house app.[24]

There are many ways to get your leader to understand the team project at first hand, and I am a big fan of getting leaders to meet their customers. It can be as simple as arranging a visit or in-person experience. Another way to involve your leader in the project is to make it a little competitive.

Tool 25

Customer quiz

A customer quiz is a great way to engage leaders in the topic, teach them something new, dispel any myths or assumptions they may have, and make them listen more. I've found that most senior people enjoy a little competition, as long as you prepare it well. This quiz draws people in and helps them to expose any assumptions they have about customers in a positive way.

How to set up a customer quiz for your leader(s):

1 What are the main things you want your leader to know or understand more about the project, customers or issue? Are there some myths that need to be busted, or assumptions that aren't quite right? Identify the main points you want to make.

2 Work out how to bring the truth to life using your customers. For example, if your team are developing an online information service for people in their seventies, and

you know that your leader thinks that anyone who's over 70 is bent over a cane, wearing tweed and playing bridge, find three 70-year-olds who are more representative of your target, for example, very fit, travel a lot or run their own business.

3   Create a basic profile of your three people with a name, age, where they live, and their job and hobbies.

4   Create five questions for them to answer that will be pertinent to the project, starting broad and then becoming more specific to the project:

- What is your favourite activity at the moment?

- What is the best thing about being able to go online?

- What are the main things you do online?

- What are your favourite apps and websites?

- Why are those your favourites?

5   Ask the customers these questions, and film them, record them or write down what they say, answering each one separately.

6   Give your leader the basic profile of each customer, and ask them to tell you what they believe the answers are, based on the limited information they have.

7   Then show them what the real answers were, by playing each answer or showing what they said on a slide.

8   End with a summary of the main things you learned from those customers (for example they all liked websites that were easy to navigate, had lots of diagrams, and allowed them to see what other people like them thought).

9   At this point you could score the answers that the leader gave, or point out where we learned something, got something completely wrong, or created more questions that need to be answered to clarify as a team.

How to use this tool:

- Be careful to set up the quiz content in advance, making sure you have the right customers answering the right types of questions that will give insights for the project.

- If you can't find or contact real customers, you can create the questions and answers using survey data or previous research, or by quoting people on social media.

- Set up the right tone in advance, making sure that the leaders expect this to be a light-hearted game, rather than a test to expose any knowledge gaps they may have.

- Play as a team or with a group of leaders, rather than making the one leader play while everyone else watches.

- Be careful that the scoring system is sound and is explained in advance, as people get very annoyed if it doesn't feel fair.

- Consider how to make it more of a game, with scorecards, multiple-choice answers or prizes to win if key phrases are used. Sometimes we even dress the quiz leader up in a sparkly jacket and act like we are on a TV show, but that's really going the extra mile.

- Make sure everyone knows that each customer is an individual to bring the topic to life and won't be fully representative of the total customer population.

Obviously, this approach won't be appropriate with all bosses, customers or topics, but you can flex it to be more suitable, such as by simply showing a statement and asking people if it's true or false, then after they have answered, talking through why they were right or wrong. One we use a lot when presenting trends is to present them as myths and then show how they are actually true (just misunderstood).

A very simple competition you can do with your team is to see how long people in the team can go without something, for example, a consumer tissue client of mine recently asked their team to go without using paper tissues and use cloth hankies instead for a few weeks, to give them an insight into the benefits of both.

Any way in which you can directly engage your leaders with the topic your team are working on will make it memorable to them, will teach them something new, and will give them something to talk about the next time.

Keeping a helicopter perspective

The best support leaders can often give is to give your team perspective. Because most bosses are not involved in the day-to-day detail, they have a wider context of how your team fits with other projects in the business. Alex Thompson, one of the world's most accomplished offshore sailors, talks about the importance of a 'helicopter view' when sailing: considering the perspective of the journey not just from the skipper's view in the cockpit, but by imagining it from the air, looking down on the boat and the journey.

The leader's perspective is invaluable to help teams come out of the day to day and consider the view from a distance. One of the main challenges we face at work is how to balance short- and long-term growth; if we are focussed too much on short-term wins, we risk not thinking ahead to what is on the horizon.[25] This might be as simple as not getting bogged down in the detail. Jennifer Whyte, Director of CMI Deodorants at Unilever, used to say to her team "The consumer is not an armpit!" to remind people working on the category to consider the consumer as a whole person, rather than just a user of deodorants.

> **Today's decision-makers are too often trapped in traditional, linear thinking, or too absorbed by the multiple crises demanding their attention, to think strategically about the forces of disruption and innovation shaping our future.**
>
> **Klaus Schwab[26]**

Decision fatigue

'Decision fatigue' happens when people have too many decisions to make. People make worse decisions when they're tired, and they are less likely to make the right ethical decision too.[27] If we draw our bosses into too many decisions, they will no longer be able to help us make the right ones. Scientists looking at how ants make decisions that affect the safety of their colony found that when an individual ant is given two choices to choose between, they take longer and make worse decisions that potentially threaten the colony. A better form of decision-making was when a group of ants explored all the possible options in parallel with each other before choosing the correct course, because of the 'choice overload' that affects an individual having to choose. In simple terms, our team is better at making decisions than giving the decision to our bosses to make.[28]

Leaders work with insufficient and incomplete information. Nobody ever has all the information they need to make a decision, and so your own personal competence is key; you need to have the ability to make judgement calls with incomplete information

Chris Hadfield[29]

Market research

Big data and big decisions

After the big filing project I talked about earlier, I worked as a market researcher at Kraft Foods, learning from my first boss and incredible mentor, Monica Juanas. We were in charge of market research for the Middle East and Africa markets, and we were responsible for delivering high-quality analysis of the market sales report. This was in the early 2000s, when the purchases and stock levels of stores across the Middle East were collected manually by field auditors in person at the stores. Because most stores selling our products did not have computers or barcode scanners, the research company would visit a representative sample of stores across each country and extrapolate likely figures for periods of two months accumulated. We got this information every two months, one month later, so we'd get January and February data by the end of March. Between finding out what had happened in the market, such as out of stock in our main selling product, or that a competitor had changed its price, implementing any changes we could, it would be more than six months before we knew if we had succeeded.

Monica still works with consumer and shopper insights, now as a strategic marketing consultant, and when we met she told me how much has changed. The supermarket data that took months to get is now delivered in ten days, so we get January's data on 10 February. This is because reports are now based on electronic point-of-sale data provided digitally by all the universe of stores, rather than extrapolated sales. In fact, if needed, it can be delivered weekly, so the first week in January could be delivered by the third week in January. However, that would be too often and would get in the way of good quality analysis and decision-making.

Monica says that the challenge is no longer availability of the information, but managing the enormous flow of information. Getting the right information to the right people at the right time in order to ensure good quality analysis is what leads to the right decisions for any business. We need to be careful that we are not fragmenting our attention, losing track of the bigger picture and reacting only to the short-term data updates. Monica told me that some teams take conscious decisions on what detail in data is shared with the different levels of responsibility, meaning that very senior leaders generally get only top-line data reports, as this is what is required for their understanding of the business and the type of decisions they need to make.

Teams can be tempted to give leaders lots of updates and share all the available information to help them share in the decision-making. However, in order to benefit from the leader's perspective, we need to keep them somewhat separate from the day to day and limit the amount of information we give them. The key is to get leaders to help us to make the right decisions, not to get them to make the decisions for us.

As we work on increasingly complex business problems, with access to more information, and the pressure to make bigger decisions more urgently, the role that leaders play is crucial to give us a 'helicopter view'. They can stand back and look for longer-term patterns, when teams are stuck in the day to day.

What matters now is not so much the quantity of data a firm can amass but its ability to connect the dots and extract value from the information.

Frank van den Driest, Stan Sthanunathan and Keith Weed[30]

Getting support from your leaders is vitally important to your team's work, but can be very challenging. The most important thing to remember is that a supercharged team gets this support – they make leaders share in deciding direction, understand what motivates them, and therefore benefit from their unique perspective to succeed.

Key take outs

- Managing up is crucial to team success.
- Understanding how your team's goals fit into the organisation's direction of travel means that your team can adapt and flex, while being sure they are travelling with the right intention.
- A leader who can see what is in the success of your project for them will help and support your team to achieve their goals.

- Building your leaders' understanding of your customers or the issues you're working on engages them further with your project.

- The perspective provided by your leaders is crucial to help your team see beyond the day to day and make the right decisions.

chapter 10

Engage your
stakeholders

Stakeholders are crucial to success. We need them to be our champions not our detractors. Many teams work on behalf of a wider group of people who have an interest in their project, and keeping those stakeholders updated can be difficult. If you give them too much information, you can get thrown off track if they interfere, but if you keep information back you risk not getting support or approvals at later stages.

Supercharged teams engage stakeholders from the start, and they keep communicating with them regularly and often through the life of the project. Use these tools to give your stakeholders regular, useful and constructive updates that keep them on side, but don't hold your team back.

What you will learn in this chapter:

- How to identify and engage your stakeholders at the beginning of the project . . .

- . . . and manage them throughout the journey.

- How to understand your stakeholders' agenda and ensure they are a positive force in the project.
- How to create a good story that stakeholders will want to share.

Who has a vested interest in your team?

The word 'stakeholder' originated in the 1700s and referred to a person who held a wager or 'that which is placed at hazard' on behalf of people gambling.[1] In other words, they were an independent person who kept the bet safe until it was clear who won it. The word has since come to mean someone who has a vested interest in your work and an interest in its success or failure.

Stakeholders can be peers in the company, or people in other departments or organisations. If you are a TV producer, your stakeholders include the commissioners who choose what goes on air. If you work in a charity, they are your trustees and clients. In the public sector, stakeholders can include voluntary organisations, community groups and residents. Anyone who might be affected by this project, and so wants to have a say in it, is a stakeholder. In most projects you know who your stakeholders are and to some extent you can choose them, although stakeholders may surprise you and choose themselves. Sometimes you have no idea people have an interest in your project until they make themselves known to you.

When I was at ITV, Europe's biggest commercial broadcaster, I worked with Clare Thompson, an expert in developing new ideas for television. We were tasked with creating big live event ideas to bring the nation together and raise money for charity. One of our best ideas was 'The Big Switch Off', which would get the whole of the UK to switch off their lights and televisions at the same time one Saturday night to raise awareness about climate change. It was only when Clare and I were contacted by the National Grid and formally invited to visit them, that we realised that they were one of our stakeholders. We spent a fascinating morning at the National Grid, being shown how the UK's electricity system worked. They explained to us how our TV event could trigger huge electricity surges and failures across the country and would be dangerous to people's safety. We canned that idea.

Managing stakeholders is a tricky balance. You need to keep them involved so they approve of what the team is doing, but if you involve them in your decision-making too much or too early, they might expect you to follow all of their advice or to include them in all your decisions. If you involve stakeholders too late for them to feel they've had any influence, they are more likely to reject your work, no matter how good it is. This is commonly called the 'not invented here' syndrome, where people are more likely to reject an idea if they have not been a part of inventing it themselves.[2] A KPMG study on innovation found that getting support from other business units is crucial to success – if the other departments are surprised by something the innovation team is working on because they weren't brought in from the start, internal clashes are likely to derail the innovation.[3]

Collaborating and communicating are hard. They're taxes. But if you're going to be successful in any large organization, you need to collaborate, whether you like it or not.

Russ Wilson[4]

While you should always have stakeholders in mind, you can't let them drive your agenda, especially because they will often be acting in their own best interests, rather than the interests of the wider group or organisation. The biggest challenge and opportunity with stakeholders is to get them to feel included enough, so that when the project is a success they share in your team's success and believe they have played a part in it.

The stakeholder journey

Engaging stakeholders is a journey, not a destination. You need to consider how and when to include them at every point in your team's progress towards your goals. Think of it as a communications campaign, starting with what you call your project, how you clarify your objectives, how you present your team, which team members contact them, how you intend to keep them involved throughout, sharing timing and deadlines, and what expectations you set from the start about how they will be involved.

The temptation at the beginning of a project is to go and talk to a couple of people about it without considering your stakeholder journey, which could raise challenges or expectations that you weren't prepared for. So, think through this journey as a team before you get any stakeholders involved.

The six stages in the stakeholder journey:

1 **Identify them:** Consider who the obvious ones are, and also whether there are any less obvious stakeholders who you might need support from later on.

2 **Update them:** Give them information about your project, its goals, your approach and how you'd like them to be involved.

3 **Understand them:** Understand what they think of the project and the approach you are taking, and what advice they have.

4 **Check in with them:** Keep them updated on your progress on a regular basis.

5 **Engage them:** Ask them for feedback and build ideas with the team.

6 **Persuade them:** Once a decision is made, persuade them it is the right one.

As a team, talk through each of the above stages together and how to prepare for them, and you will be way ahead of most project teams in planning to engage your stakeholders. The rest of this chapter will give you some approaches and tools for making your stakeholder journey even more successful.

Brand your project carefully

Before you contact stakeholders, consider what to call your project. Avoid associating your project with past failed work (so create a new project name), or build on what has been successful in the past (reuse a successful name).

I've been a workshop facilitator for two decades, and I've realised that most people have bad associations with the word 'workshop'. Because previous workshops had been badly designed and had wasted people's time, we didn't want to be associated with them. We stopped calling our sessions workshops, which is odd for me as the author of *The Workshop Book*. We name our events according to the task, so we invite people to a working session, co-creation date, insight deep dive, or accelerator meeting, any type of meeting so long as they are not attending a workshop. Be careful to make the name of your project all about the outcome, not the starting point. So instead of calling it the 'Air Pollution Committee', call it the 'Clean Air Action Group'. That changes the way you present yourselves to stakeholders from the start.

Consider a visual brand for your work. Experts estimate that at least 70% of human communication is non-verbal,[5] our attention spans are shorter, and because of the huge amount of data we are all processing, we can't just rely on words to convey the spirit of our team. Visual branding is crucial to establishing an identity and intention that other people can recognise and believe in. This can be as simple as having a particular PowerPoint template, colour scheme or even logo if you want to. These make the team and its work distinctive versus the many other projects your stakeholders come across, and becomes a short hand for them that creates its own cut-through and expectations. Are there any associations you want to avoid? If they've previously been a part of an unpopular project, consider creating a new set of materials that don't remind them of that project.

In my Project Bridge work, we have our own branding so that people recognise invitations we send – and because we are promoting people and collaboration, all our slides are simple and use visual icons, rather than looking corporate and boring with bullet points and graphs.

Allies, supporters, saboteurs

Some stakeholders will want your project to succeed and will serve as allies by giving you advice and support along the way. Others don't have a strong opinion and are happy to see what gets developed and go with it. Unfortunately, not all stakeholders will want your team to achieve your goal. If another department could have less work because you identify efficiencies, or if your work exposes old factions that you don't know about, stakeholders can become saboteurs without you even realising.

Michael Schrage asks, 'cui bono' (who benefits, who is this for) in his book *Serious Play,* and makes the point that the most powerful prototypes create winners and losers. When I read that I couldn't believe I'd never asked myself who will lose. As an optimist, I always see who might benefit, but I never think to consider who might lose – and it's the people who stand to lose who become the saboteurs, whether or not they are open about it.

One of the best things about running a small business is that I don't have to deal with the dark arts of office politics. Studies have shown that office politics, ("the observable but often covert actions through which executives influence internal decisions") have a direct, negative impact on their competitiveness and growth because it slows down the company's ability to make good decisions.[6] So, it's official – office politics is bad for business! What makes internal politics so difficult is that it is often covert. In my experience people who are excellent internal politicians don't always like workshops, because they are made to express their opinions out in the open, in front of everyone, rather than trying to influence each other separately and behind closed doors. This first tool helps you to avoid internal politics, and takes some of the power away from the internal politicians transparently and constructively.

Tool 26

Secret stakeholder survey

With this tool you anonymously survey all of your stakeholders, and compile the answers into common themes for everyone involved. Individual stakeholder interviews are a great way to understand what your stakeholders think, and definitely should be done, but a shared survey like this puts all stakeholders on an equal footing, allows them to say what they think honestly, and provides a chance for people to have their say (so that later on, they can't say that they weren't asked).

Preparing for this tool:

- Make a list of all your known stakeholders. Consider the obvious people, and include perhaps some of the senior people in the business, or other interested experts who may have valuable views. I sometimes include people who've retired, left the business or moved to new departments, as they can also give great advice.

- Compose a short survey of no more than five questions for them to answer individually and anonymously.

- Ask them to answer in as much detail as possible, as the language and emotion people use is essential to understanding their views.

- Explain that you will be quoting them verbatim (even though answers are anonymous, people are quite easily identified by what they say and how they say it, so do warn them in advance).

- Encourage people to give their opinion – they may not know the right answer, but they can give their personal view as one of many being surveyed.

- This survey works well for five to 20 people. Technically you could have any number of people answering – it makes the analysis a lot more difficult and you may need a professional researcher to help you find the main themes for more than 20 stakeholders.

Secret survey questions:

1 What are the main benefits or opportunities this project could create?

2 What are the challenges we need to overcome in this work?

3 If anything was possible, what would your wishlist be?

4 Are there any red herrings, wastes of time or dead ends we should avoid?

5 Do you have any issues and concerns about this work?

You can create your own questions to fit your project, but keep to a similar pattern (benefits, challenges, wishlist, avoids, concerns), so you are helping people to express both positives and negatives in a balanced way.

How to use this tool:

- Send the survey via an electronic survey, or ask people to handwrite answers and send to you, or simply assign one person to confidentially collate all the answers by email. The important thing is that only one person collates them, and they are anonymous – because the power of the tool is reading the answers in the common themes, not what each individual says.

- Give people a deadline to answer by. A week is the ideal deadline, any longer and people forget, any shorter and people complain they haven't been given enough notice.

- The day before the deadline remind those people who haven't yet done so to complete it and that this is their chance to have their views included.

- Once you have all the survey answers back, look at the answers to the first question, and make a note of the top three to five key themes, for example 'cost-saving' or 'improving our customer service'.

- Using PowerPoint, make a new slide for each theme. So, for example:

  - Slide 1: 'Question 1 – Theme: Cost-Saving' – put all the answers relating to cost-saving on this slide.

  - Slide 2: 'Question 1 – Theme: Improving our customer service' – put all the answers relating to improving customer service on this slide.

- Finish all the themes from Question 1, before moving on to the second question and do the same.

- Make sure you quote people in the exact language they have used, verbatim, don't summarise or reword their answers. It's important for people to read the output in their own words as part of the whole.

- You don't need to use every answer from every person, if they are similar, just make sure that the sentiment is expressed, and that each person is quoted at least a few times in the overall document.

- Some people write paragraphs, and some people write a few words. Try to select shorter quotes or single sentences from within long paragraphs to keep the answers comparable in length and to the point.

The best way to use the output of this tool is to bring people together and present it to the people who answered in one big group, perhaps as the start to a kick-off meeting about the project. If this is not possible, you can also send it out for everyone to read.

I use surveys like this on every project I do, especially in public-sector work, where we have a huge variety of interested parties, from actual politicians to residents. By asking stake-holders to share their true opinions, and by letting them see their opinions alongside other people's, they are made to consider everyone's perspectives, not just their own, and there's no chance for sneaking off for covert conversations.

This tool also works really well in teams that have more polite, guarded or introverted cultures, or for people with different languages or confidence levels because they can think about their answers and prepare them without being under pressure to say the right thing on the spot. Sometimes, and only when appropriate, we let people guess who said what, which introduces a bit of competition and fun.

Knowing what people honestly think is a great way to understand the context your team is working in at the beginning – and you can also use secret stakeholder surveys all the way through the project. This tool is a great way to make sure everyone's opinions are heard in a structured and clear way.

The biggest hurdle isn't information overload but opinion overload.

Manoush Zomorodi[7]

Building on your progress

When you share progress with your stakeholders, you risk putting your project up for criticism or challenge. When someone asks us to comment on an idea, particularly at work, it is a natural instinct to look for what's wrong with it and point that out to them. That's why in a previous company I worked for, the updates to the senior leadership teams were called 'seagulls'. You'd prepare your update slide and then the senior leaders would come in from a great height and, well, leave them covered in excrement.

Your team needs to be very careful with how you share progress with your stakeholders, because they will no doubt look for what's wrong, and won't always recognise the progress you've made as a team. If you want to make sure your stakeholders give constructive feedback and help you build better ideas, set up a building session.

Tool 27

Building session

When you have some progress to share with your stakeholders, whether it's some new ideas to decide between, or progress you've made, use this tool to make sure they build on your work, rather than simply criticise. This is important because if your team and stakeholders only focus on what is wrong, you can lose the essence of a great idea. Working out what is right about an idea, so you can keep what's good, is just as important as working out what is wrong and needs improving.

In a building session there are four steps:

1 Share ideas or progress so far.

2 Identify what is right or good with the progress so far.

3 Agree what needs improving, and suggest those improvements.

4 Share what's wrong or missing, and agree how to action.

How to run a building session:

- Bring all the stakeholders together in a meeting and talk them through the four steps of the building session, so people understand what they are going to do in the session and the time allocated to each part.
- Ask them to have pens and Post-its ready, and explain that you will be asking people to write their thoughts down

first, and wait until everyone has written, before speaking. Explain this is to get everyone's opinion (rather than just the loudest person who speaks first), and stop people from losing their own thoughts while listening to other people. It also means you can theme similar thoughts together, discussing the biggest themes first.

- Share progress or ideas so far in a structured and clear way. If there are three ideas, write them up in a similar format to each other so they are easily comparable. If there is a journey of decisions to explain, show a timeline so people follow the important points. Make it visual, as you want people to be able to refer back to your update in the next step, say by putting up flipcharts on the wall as you present.

- After you've shared progress or ideas, ask people to write out what they believe is good or right so far. Give them time to do this, with each different thought on a separate Post-it, and stick those up on a flipchart, or below the relevant idea.

- Then ask people to write what needs improving, and any ideas for making the ideas or project better, and stick those on a different flipchart or idea.

- Finally, ask people to write down what's wrong or missing, also on separate Post-its, and put those on a final flipchart.

- Split the team into three groups, one to work on the good/right thoughts, one to work on the improvements, and the last to work on what's missing/wrong.

- Ask each group to theme the Post-its from their part into similar thoughts, and summarise the key points for the rest of the group.

- Once each group has presented back, you will clearly understand where the whole stakeholder group agrees on what's good, what needs improving and what's missing.

- Once summarised, work through what needs improving, and what is missing, creating better ideas with your stakeholders together.

Setting up behaviours at the start of a build session is always important. If appropriate, I ask people not to criticise an idea, only improve it. This means that if they can't think of a better solution, the current solution stays. Putting the emphasis on building rather than criticising means people feel equally responsible for creating something with you, rather than throwing in challenges that you have to deal with. However, be careful how you use this on very difficult or emotional topics, as people want to feel like they have been heard, especially when there's no easy solution, and you don't want to close down this communication.

Building sessions can give you the right foundation to truly engage your stakeholders, making sure they build on what your team has done well, and helping you to improve the work together.

Tell good stories

More than any other attribute, this is close to the heart of the popular conception of leadership—the capacity to move people to action, to communicate persuasively, to strengthen the confidence of followers.

John Gardner[8]

When you are engaging with stakeholders, at times you will need to persuade people that you have made the right decisions. One of the best things you can do to communicate persuasively with your stakeholders is to tell them powerful stories. We remember stories far more easily than we remember facts. Think about what happens to you when someone says, "I'm going to tell you a story", we can't help but sit up and listen. Think about how to give stakeholders information about your project, not in facts and charts, but in stories they remember and want to retell to other people.

Henry Mason from TrendWatching says they are in the business of storytelling – only a small amount of work is in watching trends, mostly it is about helping to translate the information into inspiring stories that motivate client teams to innovate, change or meet new demand. In McKinsey's Building Blocks of Change model that we use in our behaviour change work, the first stage of creating successful behaviour change is starting with a compelling story.[9] Engagement is about participating or being involved in something, and there is an art to making your stakeholders feel that they are a part of your project's story.

Women and swimsuits

Many women love swimming, but they only love swimming when they get into the water and actually swim. Everything else, from undressing in a public changing room, to putting on a swimsuit that reveals your body to total strangers, to the public catwalk you have to walk to get into the swimming pool, to wearing a wetter, tighter swimsuit on the way back to the changing rooms where everyone sees your back view, to changing in public changing rooms again is far from enjoyable. I'm sure many women will identify with this, but the mostly male board of decision-makers at a swimwear company I was working with didn't really get it. They believed women were a bit uncomfortable, but they couldn't understand the level of discomfort, self-consciousness and dread their customers felt.

We asked everyone on the team to talk to friends and family members, and one quote we heard was "I'm so self-conscious about the way I look in my swimming costume that I literally lose the ability to walk properly". This quote carried all the emotion that connected the team more deeply with their customers, and they had this in mind in every innovation decision they then made. A simple, one sentence story like this carried a powerful message, and was easy for people to retell to people outside the team to help them to understand too.

When you're engaging stakeholders, supercharged teams tell stories that are so memorable that they become new currency, as good as a news story that you want to be the first to tell to others about because you are passing on something valuable.

How organisations enact ideas – not the ideas themselves – is the soul and substance of innovation.

Michael Schrage[10]

The elevator pitch

Because stakeholder engagement is a communication journey, think about how to make the story of your project single-minded, focussed and easy to remember and repeat. What do you want your stakeholders to say when they are asked in the lift about the project, that can be said in the time it takes to travel between floors? What is your team's elevator pitch? As a team, consciously create the one-sentence description of your project that you will repeat in every single communication, to keep your stakeholders on track.

Adrian Bleasdale, COO of Horizon Platforms, is a project management specialist who told me that by far the most important ingredient of success for some of his biggest and most challenging projects was regular communication with stakeholders, beyond even creating roadmaps or tracking actions. During COVID-19, they moved from weekly and monthly stakeholder updates to daily or twice daily communications, often repeating the same messages several times to ensure it was clear and consistent.

In the end, the ideal stakeholder engagement is when they claim your team's success as their own. This means they need their own story to tell about their role in your project. What will your stakeholder say when people ask them about how your project was so successful? How will they talk about their role in your success? Make telling a positive story about your team as easy as possible for your stakeholders.

Good stories always beat good spreadsheets.

Chris Sacca[11]

Tool 28

Start well, end well

Only pessimism sounds profound. Optimism sounds superficial.

Teresa Amabile[12]

A study of business people proved that people seem more intelligent if they are critical, and less intelligent when positive or optimistic. So, you can understand why it is so tempting for stakeholders to show cleverness by criticising. That's why we often need to make sure we are not only getting the pessimistic view from the 'clever put-down artists'.[13] How we use language in meetings with stakeholders can mean the difference between success and failure – if all we hear is the negatives, what hope does the project have of progressing?

The last tool is a very simple one. When meeting with your stakeholders, make sure you start and end the interaction constructively. This is a deceptively simple tool that I use in every meeting I run. Ask for a positive and negative comment at the start of a meeting, and again at the end.

- **Start well:** At the start of a meeting, ask every stakeholder to answer two questions:
  - What are you looking forward to today?
  - What concerns would you like us to cover today?

- **End well:** At the end of a meeting, ask each stakeholder to answer two questions:
  - What have we achieved today?
  - What are you still concerned about?

How to use this tool:

- Warn your stakeholders you will be asking the 'start well' questions in advance, as some people like to be prepared, especially if they are not confident or don't like being put on the spot. No need to warn them about the 'end well' questions – better to have that one as part of the meeting.

- At the very beginning of the meeting, after going over the agenda, ask everyone in the meeting – stakeholders and your team – to answer both start well questions before any updates or discussions.

- This is a great way to get a 'temperature check' in the room, especially if you've not met everyone before. You can immediately understand people's attitudes in how they answer both questions, and it puts everyone, team and stakeholders, on an equal footing with each other as they all know what each other's feelings, intentions and concerns are from the start.

- Write down people's answers on a flipchart and refer back to them at the end of the meeting to check that you covered their issues at the end, and if not agree to do so later.

- At the end of the meeting, allow enough time to ask every person in turn to answer the end well questions, stakeholders and team members again. I cannot stress how important this is – if you have time pressure and you have to choose, choose the 'end well' questions.

- The reason why it works so well is that it asks people to acknowledge what has been achieved, and you'll be surprised at how motivating it is to hear different people's views on what progress has been made. Just hearing people's answers makes them all feel a lot more positive than they would going away with just their view.

- You also give people a structured chance to say what they are concerned about – which encourages people to express their worries openly, rather than covertly later.

- You can write down the 'end well' answers too, and refer to them when planning the next meeting.

- Please use the correct wording when you ask the questions, don't summarise them down to "everyone say one positive and one negative". The way you ask the questions helps people to answer them usefully and constructively.

It is no exaggeration to say I use this tool in every meeting and workshop I run. Helping people to start and end well frames the whole meeting between two balanced and constructive pillars that bring people together and help them understand each other better.

Stakeholders are vital to success

No matter how brilliant you make something, if people don't feel a part of it, they will reject it as 'not invented here'. Successfully engaging stakeholders is a balance between giving them as much information as they need to feel included and positive about your team and its work, without giving away too much. A supercharged team wins stakeholders' hearts and minds, and gives the project the best chance of success.

Key take outs

- When it comes to stakeholders, look beyond the obvious.
- Your stakeholders are a necessary part of your project journey, and you need to take them with you.
- Investing time in understanding your stakeholders' agenda and giving them opportunities to be heard and participate in the project are key factors in its success.
- How you brand and tell the story of your project are important factors in engaging your stakeholders, and helping them to engage others.

chapter 11

Build a new culture

The difference between an average team and a supercharged team is their ability to recognise the culture they work in and influence it. We all work in a culture, whether that is the type of business, the organisation, the department they work in, or the location. The culture of that environment has a huge impact on what the team achieves. When people say "This is how things are done around here", they are referring to their working culture, which is made up of all the processes, values and goals of the people in it, how they work together, and even how it looks and feels to work there.[1]

Supercharged teams are aware of and navigate the company culture, either by working well within that culture, or working to change the culture to make the goal achievable.

What you will learn in this chapter:

- How to understand the culture your team is working in.
- How to achieve your goal within a culture that won't change.
- How to change the culture in order to achieve your team's goal.

Culture has a powerful influence on a team

Culture eats strategy for breakfast.

Peter Drucker (1909–2005)

Culture is not changed easily, and cultural issues can't be avoided. Your team can have excellent new ideas, and all the best evidence for change, but if your team's goals don't fit the current culture, the work may not succeed. A 2019 survey of 215 corporate innovators found that the main challenges to successfully rolling out ideas to their company or market were company culture and entrenched attitudes.[2]

As a consultant, I see lots of different company cultures and I am fascinated by how different they are. Here are some I have come across:

- **Get everyone's opinion:** A very creative business in which every decision is discussed in detail with anyone who has an opinion on it, before everyone finally agrees. There is no rushing this, and unless people feel they have heard all views, no progress is made. This means it takes a long time to create something that everyone agrees with, but when they do the work is excellent and everyone feels a part of it.

- **Ownership mindset:** A consumer goods company that behaves like entrepreneurs by staying lean and agile, not wasting money and being efficient. People who work there are relentlessly competitive even with each other, and don't need to agree before they take their own decisions. Because they are very reactive, they 'pivot' (change direction on decisions) quite often, without needing to get alignment from their wider team, so they move quicker than competitors.

- **Best-practice theorists:** A large global client of mine likes to do things properly, and has always seen itself as defining the best practice in the industry. Its systems and processes are excellent, but I often hear them jokingly saying "That's all very well in practice, but how does it look in theory?", as they tend to want to codify everything into a toolkit to teach to others.

- **Careful decisions department:** In the public sector, when people are working on complex issues like child protection or public health, decisions are made very carefully because of the consequences of getting it wrong. It can mean projects take months rather than weeks to complete due to assessing all the risks and making sure vulnerable people's needs are fully met.

Why does culture matter for teams? If what you are trying to achieve is contrary to the current culture, you can be the best team in the world, but your work will not land. If you want people to do something new and quickly, but they are used to discussing and agreeing with everyone first, they will find it hard to change. If you want to promote a culture of collaboration, but people are used to competing with each other, they won't behave differently just because your team asks them to.

If what your team wants does not fit within the culture, you need to change how you achieve your goal, or make changing the culture your goal.

Accept the culture, change how you achieve your goal

Most teams have to achieve their goals within a culture, instead of trying to change it. This doesn't mean ignoring the culture and moving ahead anyway. It means considering how it impacts on the team's goals, barriers to overcome, and how to prepare the best approach. To do this teams must understand the culture they work in more deeply. Culture can be unconscious, and people may not realise that things are different in other places. To really understand a culture, the team needs to delve into the underlying assumptions that determine how its members perceive, think and feel.[3]

There are these two young fish swimming along, and they happen to meet an older fish swimming the other way, who nods at them and says, "Morning, boys, how's the water?" And the two young fish swim on for a bit, and then eventually one of them looks over at the other and goes, "What the hell is water?"

David Foster Wallace (1962–2008)

David Wallace's point is that the most obvious, important realities can be the ones that are the hardest to see and talk about. Culture can be so obvious that we take it for granted, but we need to consider what it means for our team. In her book *The Culture Map*, Erin Meyer talks about 'reading the air' as a way of reading a culture you are working in. She mentions hearing her Japanese colleagues referring to 'kuuki yomenai', as 'one who cannot read the air', or someone who is not good at reading between the lines. We need to be able to read the air of the culture we are working in, even if the culture we are working in is, to us, like water – we don't even realise we are in it. This tool will help you to read between the lines.

Tool 29

Code your culture

A great way to code the culture your team is working in is to ask what shapes the culture, and why this is the case. This helps you to identify the possible barriers for your team's work landing well, and the opportunities for your team to increase their chances of success.

There are four main questions the team can ask themselves to code the culture they are working in:

1 What do people value in this culture? What is held to be true, what is publicly and privately valued, and who is admired and why?

2 How do people behave? What are the common behaviours we see, how do people work with each other, and what is considered acceptable or unacceptable behaviour, and why?

3 How do people communicate? What kinds of language do people use, and how do they share information and talk with each other, and why is this?

4 How and where do people work? What are the different locations, spaces or logistics issues that influence the culture here, and why?

If you reflect on each of these questions as a team, you will identify the barriers and therefore opportunities for your team's work to succeed within the culture. Use this tool by answering each of the four questions in turn, considering as a team what people care about, why, barriers that might pose us for our team, and opportunities for overcoming these.

Here's an example showing how the tool works.

Example:
Code Your Culture

- -

Example team goal: To increase collaboration across different departments and share advice and best practice with each other more easily.

Example business culture: Ownership mindset (from the list above)

1. Culture codes	2. What do people do?	3. Why do they do this?	4. Barriers for our collaboration project	5. Opportunities for our team to help people collaborate more in this company culture
What do people value?	Quick, decision-making, as if they own the company and are spending their own money.	They don't like to waste time or money, and they actively fight against anything that slows them down, sounds bureaucratic or takes away their individual power to make decisions.	When people hear 'collaboration' they think it's a waste of time and money, and they worry they will be forced to be nice to people around them but this will have no real business impact.	Ban the word 'collaboration' – call the project 'peer mentors' from now on. Get senior leaders to recognise and reward peer-sharing, showing how it leads to business results. Measure its impact on the business to show evidence that working together makes money.
How do people behave?	People are honest and challenging, and openly competitive with each other. They respect strong views and clever thinking.	As long as you are getting the best results for the company, you don't need to be polite – the people who do well here are high performers who are not easily offended.	People don't want to share their ideas with other people who could steal them. They want to stand out as individuals rather than as part of a good team.	Set up a competition where individuals win prizes for their peer mentor successes and showcase how they created business impact through challenging their peers (thereby sharing information). Continue to encourage constructive conflict at all levels.

1. Culture codes	2. What do people do?	3. Why do they do this?	4. Barriers for our collaboration project	5. Opportunities for our team to help people collaborate more in this company culture
How do people communicate?	Mostly via WhatsApp/ Slack or very short emails, no big face-to-face meetings or workshops.	Decisions are made quickly and in the moment, and they move fast. They don't want long presentations or workshops.	Unless we can help people to collaborate better in the platforms they are already using, we won't have any influence. Setting up a collaboration workshop or new database for information sharing won't work as people won't turn up.	Create a mobile app that allows people to easily copy, paste and share crucial information with a wider 'peer mentor' audience. Encourage reviews, likes and ratings, so people get immediate feedback and encouragement that their collaboration is valued and visible at an individual level.
How and where do people work?	They travel a lot, and are always working on the move. People are hot-desking and don't have meeting rooms or private offices.	Because so many people travel and work in several locations, the office spaces are all set up for informal, water cooler-type conversations, rather than formal meetings.	Any collaboration tools or behaviours need to work remotely, and can't rely on big face-to-face meetings or presentations.	Create a series of 'peer mentor' podcasts where people talk through great case studies and best practice and give each other advice that can be listened to on the move by a wider audience.

For the above illustration, the team's project goal of increasing collaboration across different departments has some major challenges, starting with the word 'collaboration'. The language an organisation uses carries so much of its culture. A huge part of working with a new client is knowing and understanding the language it uses. Always ask early on if you don't understand a word or phrase that is commonly used – rather than finding yourself a year down the line using a TLA (three-letter acronym) wishing you knew what it stood for. Using this tool helps us to understand and accept the culture we are working in, and adapt the work to give us the best chance of achieving our team's goal.

Keep the goal, change the culture

High performance cultures need to be managed.

Michael Schrage[4]

Great company cultures are not a happy accident – they are deliberately created, encouraged, and reinforced by everyone in the organisation. I get to work with some of the best company cultures in the world, and in every experience, from how you are greeted at the offices to the tone of voice on the products, to how people show up in meetings, to what the bathrooms look like, is a part of a powerful culture that they have created.

Netflix

Freedom and responsibility

There is also no clothing policy at Netflix, but no one has come to work naked lately.

Patty McCord[5]

Netflix's culture is based on freedom and responsibility. Employees are trusted to behave as adults, and there's an expectation that they will take responsibility for their actions. As a result, they have no 9 to 5 policy, no vacation policy, and their expenses, entertainment or travel policy is five words long: Act in Netflix's best interests.

Courage and integrity are amongst the company's core values. Employees are encouraged to say what they think, even if it is uncomfortable. The company works hard to get people to give each other professional, constructive feedback on a continual basis. The company invests time in developing these professional relationships, and helps people to learn how to give and receive feedback through coaching and modelling the behaviours it wants to see in every employee.

Pret a Manger

Happy teams, happy customers, happy business

Pret launched in 1984 with an aim to deliver simple, delicious food served by friendly, motivated staff, and I've been a customer since I first moved to London in 1999. What is always noticeable, even now they have grown to 450 shops in nine countries, is the people. Whether at an airport at 5am or in the big flagship shop in Covent Garden, Pret people behave differently – they are friendly, welcoming and energetic. I'll never forget the first time I forgot my wallet and was given a free coffee anyway. Andrea Wareham, Director of HR, told me Pret's big secret is that they only hire people with a strong desire and ability to connect with other people.

Andrea calls these people 'low ego, high care', and even the leaders they recruit must prove they can practise thoughtful leadership. They are very careful to get those hires right, and make no exceptions. These values are seen in every other aspect of the business. So there are no private offices even for the senior team, people work open plan so they can chat and connect, and every person in the business has time working on the shop floor alongside frontline staff every year.[6]

Kinship

Building a pet-friendly culture

Around the globe, pets are becoming more and more important to people – 87% of owners now say they treat their pets like family. Mars, one of the world's biggest food companies, recognised this growing opportunity and created an independent company called Kinship to support start-ups in pet-related technology and innovation.

Kinship's purpose is to improve pets' lives, and this permeates every single aspect of the company's culture. Staff are not only allowed, but encouraged to bring their pets to work, and can take parental leave to welcome a new pet to the family. Even the language used by the business has pets in mind: pet owners are Pet Parents, and projects include Pet Project (a pitch event for innovators) and Companion Fund (an investment fund for pet care businesses). Keeping pets happy doesn't just keep customers happy, it makes Kinship's employees happy too.

What do these three examples of great culture have in common? Even though culture can be experienced in everything from the way the offices look to the services they produce, the culture is upheld by people – what they value, how they feel, and the stories they tell about the business, the rules of engagement they set, the language they use. 'The way we do things around here' is a story, and the business needs a strong, single-minded story to keep people and their culture on track.

The important thing about culture is you have to set it, restate it, and work through issues with the culture in mind.

Tool 30

Create your culture

Many successful team outcomes will require people to change. Whether understanding customers in a new way, or adopting new ideas, or working differently, teams often need to help people to change what they are used to doing. It is very difficult to change people and their culture. There are entire industries dedicated to culture and behaviour change, and if you are trying to change the culture of an entire business, you will need to have a team dedicated to it, usually with some specialist help.

However, if you want to begin culture change with your team, there are small, pragmatic steps that can be taken, which do work.

There are five steps to this tool as follows:

1 **Code the culture:** Use Tool 29 above to consider as a team who you are working with, the barriers you might face, and ideas to overcome these.

2 **Tell the story:** Come up with a short simple story about why we need to change our culture or behaviours. Make sure this story is memorable, can be retold by everyone who hears it, and is repeated many times.

3 **Set expectations:** Make clear what the new expectations are in specific details, supported by new tools, checklists or processes.

4 **Lead by example:** Make sure that every senior person and all team members know how to exhibit the behaviours and culture you want to achieve, and do so constantly.

5 **Repeat and reinforce:** Keep doing these five steps repeatedly until people understand the story, know what's

expected, see other people doing it, and experience it repeatedly in every experience. You will need to keep doing this for far longer than you think, and you will see progress.

Example:
Create Your Culture

- -

Here's an example of a simple culture change to show you how the tool can work.

Example team goal: To stop people from arriving late to meetings

1. Code the culture	People are used to arriving five to ten minutes late for every meeting. This is because they are in back-to-back meetings, and haven't booked time to grab a drink, go to the toilet or check urgent emails. Barriers to changing this are that it feels out of people's control – they don't mean to be late, they just can't help it, and they are under pressure to accept all the meetings they are invited to
2. Tell the story	Ask the boss to record a short film to go out company-wide, talking to people about the need to be more realistic with each other's time, respectful of the workloads we each have, and the importance of not keeping people waiting as this can waste each other's time.

3. Set expectations	Set out three new meeting booking rules for everyone in the company to commit to: 1. Change all meetings from 60 minutes to 45 minutes, starting on the hour, but leaving 15 minutes as a break between one meeting and the next, for every meeting, for the whole company. 2. Ask people to start meetings on time, even if some are running late, rather than wait (and catch up latecomers at the end). 3. Ask people to take control of their diaries and make sure they have 15 minutes between meetings, arrive at meetings on time, and give them permission to not accept meetings that don't allow 15 minutes between each.
4. Lead by example	Ask the boss to change all their meetings for the next month to reflect the new timings, and share the impact of that (good and bad) at the end of each week in a short update film.
5. Repeat and reinforce	Give every meeting organiser a short checklist to go through when setting up every meeting, asking people attending to clear time in advance so they start on time, and then making sure meetings start on time, and catching up anyone who could not avoid arriving late after the meeting ends. Ask meeting organisers to fill in a short survey on success of this for every meeting and track over time whether scores improve.

The above steps are both simple and profoundly challenging. Your team must make sure they are constantly revisiting the culture change to reinforce it.

Project Bridge

Changing the culture of a city

I live in Portsmouth, a coastal city on the south coast of the UK. We have a strong economy and cultural heritage, but like most cities we have poverty and social issues which are too complicated to be solved by just one organisation alone. Research tells us that collaboration helps organisations and individuals deliver good outcomes locally,[7] and over the last few years we have developed a culture change toolkit called Project Bridge that helps the public, voluntary and private sectors in our city to work together with residents.

As a result, we have made progress on some of the city's biggest issues, including reducing the rough sleepers on our streets, raising awareness of how to protect children against criminal and sexual exploitation, and preventing childhood obesity by working with schools and families to encourage healthy eating and exercise.

Project Bridge created a collaboration culture in Portsmouth with specific rules of engagement:

- People from different organisations come together to work on complex issues, including local government, health, charities, businesses and community members.

- We build trust and relationships first by creating a shared vision of a successful future outcome together, before discussing ideas or funding.

- Everyone is an equal partner, so we work without hierarchy or political agendas when we collaborate.

- We co-create ideas with people who have lived experience, so that the people of Portsmouth are at the centre of all initiatives and decisions.

- We ask people to use normal language, and avoid acronyms, official terminology and complicated jargon.

- We ask for a constructive mindset, which means that people build on each other's ideas, and if they don't like an idea they come up with a better one instead of rejecting it without an alternative.

- When initiatives are agreed, funding goes to projects based on cross-organisational collaborations so that local partnerships and networks are strengthened.

Portsmouth City Councillor Steve Pitt told me, "Having a culture of collaboration means we can work together in the community to solve the issues that affect us all. When we do things with people, not to people, we know it means better outcomes for everyone living in our city." Project Bridge is a best-practice method for community collaboration that is now being used across the UK.

Culture change is more important, and more difficult than ever before

Culture: from the Latin cultus, which means care.

Daniel Coyle[8]

We are living in a time of unprecedented change, and to work within this change will inevitably mean we must change our culture, to either accept and work within what is happening, or to improve and evolve our work to make the most of new opportunities. Whether it is the result of digital transformation, market disruption, more complex world issues, customer behaviour change or employee attitudes shifting, we will all need to change our culture.

Ipsos MORI

Lessons from lockdown

COVID-19 forced many companies to change their culture and with that came positive lessons. Ben Page, CEO of Ipsos MORI UK and Ireland, told me that political leaders across Europe had experienced double-digit approval ratings growth early in the crisis, both because leaders tend to communicate more often and more effectively in times of crisis, but also because voters 'rally round the flag' at times of national emergency. I found this in the UK, where the daily TV updates allowed us to get to know our cabinet members better.

Ben experienced this in his own business too. Ipsos MORI has 1,500 employees, and before COVID-19 Ben used to do a quarterly presentation to all employees across the country, in person. After lockdown, he began a 20-minute weekly update for all employees online, which has turned out to be more effective. Because video calls allowed Ben to connect directly with everyone, he could reassure and lead his teams in person, at scale. As business leaders take their lessons from lockdown back into the post-COVID-19 recovery, Ben believes our opportunity is to keep the best bits and learn from them – and certainly he plans to keep doing the 20-minute weekly update where possible.

Unfortunately, the pace of change means people are already experiencing 'change fatigue', which can cause resistance to transformation, a decline of employee trust and possible burnout for some.[9] Even though culture change is hard, and people are resistant to it, we should not stop caring about creating the right culture.

Supercharged Teams is really a book about supercharging culture change, starting with what you can control, your team and the people on those teams, and eventually having an impact on the wider environment they work in. Culture change is a necessity, not a choice, and the sooner we start to approach it, no matter how challenging, the earlier we will create the right culture we want to work in for ourselves, our teams and our companies. Culture change is a long journey. Keep going, far longer than you think, and you will get there.

Key take outs

- Company cultures are many and varied – understanding the culture in which your team is working is critical to achieving your team's goal.

- Culture change is not a quick fix, but can be achieved through commitment and consistently putting it into practice.

chapter 12

What do teams look like in the future?

Teams will be even more important in future, and supercharged teams are the only ones that will succeed. The National Research Council found that when companies are dealing with unclear goals and uncertain markets, teamwork is more important to success than ever before.[1]

> **We always overestimate the change that will occur in the next two years and underestimate the change that will occur in the next ten. Don't let yourself be lulled into inaction.**
>
> **Bill Gates[2]**

Artificial intelligence will measure our performance and help us to improve, whether as a team member, or as a team, or as the organisation itself, and will help us identify new opportunities quickly. We may be overwhelmed with information for decision-making, and will need to prioritise faster, better decisions and avoid data paralysis. We are likely to face a high turnover of team members to bring in the expertise to deal with market disruption, and because gig-style working means people won't be permanent. Team rules of engagement will be continually reset to keep us on course, so supercharging your team regularly will be a necessity not a choice.

We will need to preserve and value what people bring in a world that is increasingly machine-led. We will need human-machine collaboration to get the best results. We will need to constantly evolve, both as individuals and as teams.

In the end, it all comes down to people and values. We need to shape a future that works for all of us by putting people first and empowering them.

Klaus Schwab[3]

What you will learn in this chapter:

- How teams of the future will include machines . . .
- . . . and our customers.
- How teams will continually evolve and develop.
- What will drive our teams in future.

Machines will join our teams

Artificial intelligence (AI) is when we create technology systems that can function intelligently and independently. Experts agree that while AI will take on the heavy lifting of data analysis and scenario planning, the key challenge is how we help humans to make better, cleverer decisions with that information. To put it another way, we will need to collaborate with machines to make decisions together.

It's fair to say AI will increasingly take on routine and repetitious tasks. That means it'll be up to teams of humans to assess the options AI provides, but also build on those options with intuitive, creative, non-standard solutions.

Greg Orme[4]

Pedro Uria-Recio Group Head of Analytics and Artificial Intelligence at Axiata, one of Asia's leading telecommunications groups, says that it is collaboration between humans and machines that will increase our performance in future. According to Harvard research, while AI algorithms can read medical diagnostic scans with 92% accuracy, and humans can do the same with 96% accuracy, working together they can achieve 99% accuracy.

Future teams will need to use data to make creative, innovative and intelligent decisions. Emotional intelligence, creativity and persuasion will become all the more valuable in future to facilitate teamwork and good decision-making.[5] Team–machine collaboration will become core to a great team.

Customers will join our teams

We are already seeing a massive increase in the importance of transparency across brands and business. More than ever, consumers require the businesses they support and work for to be ethically sound.[6]

Consumers are getting involved, both alongside and increasingly in the place of, brands. Increasingly aware that personality, purpose and profit can be compatible, consumers seek brands with meaning and character; that are open, honest, sympathetic, and, most importantly, stand for something.

Henry Mason[7]

Information that used to be hard to find will increasingly be accessed and communicated by our customers, and even our own competitors. In a climate of radical transparency, instead of keeping our projects a secret from our customers, we will involve them in our decision-making. This is already being done by companies like Coca-Cola, which brings in its retail and restaurant customers to help it create more relevant products together, from the KOLab Innovation Centre at the Atlanta HQ.[8]

In future, augmented by collaboration platforms, we will be able to engage our customers to help us at every stage of a project journey to make sure they have a say in the decisions we take. Truly open innovation in the public and private sector will mean we need to balance between what the team wants to achieve, and how to qualify and improve that by consumer involvement. This is not being told what consumers want. As Henry Ford said, "If I had asked people what they wanted, they would have said faster horses." Consumers can't direct what they want, but by involving people at every stage to test and learn, we can make products and services that are a perfect fit to customers' needs.

We will evolve to thrive

As team members, we will be able to measure our own performance, from how we interact, the hours we work, and how big our network is, to the effectiveness of our personal performance on the company profit. We will be guided by self-improvement at home and at work.

Microsoft already provides users with a productivity score based on the data it collects about how you work when using its systems.[9] There is already a trend in constant learning and self-improvement at work, with one study finding that 83% of employees see keeping their skills up-to-date as their responsibility rather than the company's, and 51% willing to take on an internal gig to gain experience.[10] This fits with a growing desire people will have to improve their health, their knowledge, and their skills away from work too.[11]

Michael Schrage says our 'selvesware' (the digital tools we use to help us manage our multiple roles in life, both professional and personal) will give us advice on how we can improve our performance, collaboration, efficiency and productivity within these different roles, and he calls this 'augmented introspection'.[12]

More and more people are being chosen for elite sports teams based not only on their existing talent but their ability to be coached, to be improved, to learn from the performance data. Choose people for your team who are open to learning, measurement, who will choose to improve and evolve. Average is over.

Michael Schrage[13]

In the Pareto principle, or the 80/20 rule, it is argued that 20% of our work results in 80% of the impact we make.[14] For example, we overestimate the importance of answering all of our emails (which could take up 80% of our time), not realising that it might be the water cooler chat with our boss that had the most impact on our successful decision-making (the 20%). In future, we will be able to trace all of our impact back to the specific actions we took, and our selvesware will advise us to create more water cooler moments and spend less time answering emails.

For future teams, optimised individual and team performance will be the basic expectation of joining a team. People will be chosen for teams not only based on past evidence of performance and their ability to contribute to teamwork, but also their ability to learn and improve on the job. Their performance, and the performance of the whole team will be tracked and measured and constantly sharpened to get the best results for the business.

This means future teams will focus on nurturing agility, adaptability and re-skilling team members.

Teams and machines will be driven by a sense of purpose

We will continue to rely on human creativity, insight and collaboration to achieve the best results, even in a machine-led world. Companies will be challenged to be ethical by their customers, because it is increasingly difficult for them to hide unethical practices or how they treat their teams.

People are becoming more driven by purpose at work.[15] In future our need for purpose-driven work will not only accelerate, it will also become more possible. Meaning may come from the team's ethical objectives, the feeling of belonging to a team, the investment offered in learning and self-improvement, or the way the teamwork fits around other personal projects.

Teams will be the human experience that people seek and enjoy, because they are freed by technology to focus on the uniquely human. Because AI frees up time that would otherwise be spent on data-crunching, repetitive tasks or analysis, people will have more time to work together better.

Henry Mason, author of *Trend Driven Innovation* says it's not just that AI will free us up to do better work, but that 'beneficial intelligence' will deliver more ethical outcomes. Walt Disney is already using AI to analyse scripts to identify gender bias, and the United Nations World Food Programme can identify real-time food needs based on public information. AI gives us a huge opportunity to make each other's lives better too.

Organizations will become more collaborative and increasingly agile and nonhierarchical. Higher employee satisfaction, more creativity, more free time, reduced employee churn, and increased customer satisfaction will be some of the positive consequences of AI in the workplace. AI will make the workplace more human, not less. This is the gift of AI to mankind.

Pedro Uria-Reco[16]

Teams will need to keep supercharging

The future is already here – it's just unevenly distributed.

William Gibson[17]

Today, and in the future, we cannot keep working in the same way we always have, only faster, hoping to keep up. We will no longer be able to accept inherited team cultures or team members who do not directly contribute to our impact. We need to reassess and reset how our teams work.

Supercharged teams will be an imperative rather than a choice, the only way to keep up with the evolving demands of work, data and technology. This book gives you the permission and the tools to reset your team, and create your best possible future success.

Key take outs

- -

- In the future our team members will include artificial intelligence . . .
- . . . and our customers will be key members of our teams too.
- To keep thriving teams will continually learn and develop new skills . . .
- . . . and be driven by an ever-greater sense of purpose.
- Crucially, teams will keep supercharging!

chapter 13

Using *Supercharged Teams* and the 30 tools in your team

Whether you are working in a small or large team, face to face, in the same building or across the world from each other, this set of tools will help you as a team member or leader to reset your ways of working and achieve your goals by becoming a supercharged team.

It is up to you to use the tools in the way you feel will suit your team – there are no hard and fast rules. Each tool is intended to be useful as a stand-alone, and can be used as and when they are necessary. When you read the overview of the 30 tools (summarised here for your reference), you may already know which ones your team needs most. However, there are some that should be done in order. For example, you need to choose your team and set a goal before you agree what you will deliver and when.

What you will learn in this chapter:

- How to use the 30 tools to supercharge your team.
- How to decide which areas to focus on.

- How to diagnose your team's strengths and areas for improvement.
- How to plan your supercharged teams workshop.

How to use the 30 tools

Chapter by chapter

When you create or join a team, agree to work through the book, chapter by chapter together. On a weekly or monthly basis, everyone in the team will read the same chapter, and decide which tool or tools are relevant for your team. Depending on the issues you want to cover and the time you have, set aside either a few hours, half a day or a full day to work these through. Ask different people in the team to volunteer to run each tool, rotating the facilitator role in turn so that everyone has a chance to prepare and lead an exercise, and have that same person be responsible for writing up the results and sending them to the team within a few days.

Prioritised issues

If you are in an existing team and there's a particular issue that needs resolving, identify the chapters you need to focus on. You can do this by asking every member of the team to read Chapter 1 and be ready to say the top two chapters, issues or tools they believe the team needs to focus on. Get the team to write their top two or three points on separate Post-its and share them in a team meeting, grouping similar answers together. Start by working on the area, chapter or tool with the most mentions.

One-off tools

If you're in a team that's working well and there's no immediate issue to sort out, keep re-evaluating and resetting by choosing a tool to use each week or month as an energiser, team exercise or break from the team's work. Give each person in the team the chance to choose the tool they want to do per meeting, making sure everyone in the team gets a chance to choose. Or, choose the tool randomly by asking someone to pick a number between 1 and 30 out of a hat, or ask your leader or stakeholder to pick a tool for the team to work on. The important thing is to always keep resetting your team, don't stop. Things change, and the tools help you to keep the team fit for purpose and supercharged.

How to choose what to work on in your team

If it's not immediately clear to you which tools your team will most benefit from, use this guide to help you choose. *Supercharged Teams* tools fall into four need areas:

1 A strong foundation for teamwork:
   * Chapter 2: Choose your team
   * Chapter 3: Find more time
2 Planning for success
   * Chapter 4: What goals do you want to achieve?
   * Chapter 5: Find your motivation
   * Chapter 6: Agree what you will deliver, and when
3 How we behave together
   * Chapter 7: Ways to work together
   * Chapter 8: Dealing with conflict
4 Increasing our chances of success
   * Chapter 9: Get support from leaders
   * Chapter 10: Engage your stakeholders
   * Chapter 11: Build a new culture

As a team you may choose to focus on the main issues first, doing those tools, then coming back to the others as relevant. You could choose to focus on the tools in one need area only, or work on more.

If you're not sure which area to focus on, you may find it useful to ask the team to decide using some team diagnostic questions.

Diagnostic questions

Ask your team, leaders and stakeholders to answer these questions to identify your team's strengths and where there's room for improvement in each area. Discuss each of these questions as a team before deciding which specific tools to use, or send these out in advance and ask team members to share their thoughts beforehand, combining the answers into themes that you then work through.

The foundations of great teamwork:

- Do we need a team, do we have the right people in our team, do we have enough time to fully participate and are we motivated enough to achieve what we want to?
- What are the strong foundations this team already has?
- What do we need to do to improve the foundations of teamwork in this team?

Planning for success:

- Do we know what we want to achieve, the project scope and how we will get there? Are we clear on outcomes, timing and deliverables?
- Where are we aligned on what we want to achieve, and how?
- What do we need to improve our vision, goals, roadmap or alignment?

How we behave together:

- Have we clearly, deliberately and openly agreed the rules of engagement our team commits to that will help us to work together well? Are we clear how we will deal with or avoid conflict?
- What are the strengths, talents and ways of working that help this team work well together?
- What are the small and bigger issues we need to resolve or plan for?

Increasing our chances of success:

- Do we have the right support we need from our leaders, and have we considered how to keep our stakeholders involved? Are we aware of the culture we work in and how that will affect our teamwork?

- What will help us to keep leaders, stakeholders and the wider business on side?

- What do we need to consider to anticipate any issues with leaders, stakeholders or the organisation if we want to succeed?

Once you know which areas you want to focus on, and the order of importance, plan a team workshop to use the tools in.

Supercharged team workshops

Depending on the time you have and the importance or urgency of the issue, consider the amount of time you have for a team workshop to run some or all of the tools you need in your team.

If you are working on a complicated project, allowing one full day to plan for success will definitely be worth the time you spend by saving you from setting off in the wrong direction. If there is a major issue that needs sorting out, but you have limited time, it is better to do something in two hours next week than wait a month for the time to do a four-hour session. If you can plan to do a two-hour workshop as soon as possible, then a four-hour session later on, it means you can decide closer to the time how to use the four hours well.

Here are four possible supercharged team workshop lengths, along with guidelines of how much you can achieve in each session:

Two-hour workshop

- One chapter, and one tool.
- Prep work for each team member will take 30 minutes (to be completed before the session).

- Share the prep work in the session and identify key themes, ideas and ways forward.
- Agree who will action the outputs.

Half-day workshop

- One chapter and two tools, or two chapters, one tool from each.
- Prep work for each team member will take 60 minutes before the session, 30 minutes per tool, for two different prep work tasks.
- Consider how to order the session so that the first tool creates a good starting point for the next. For example, use Tool 8 'Reframe your aim' followed by Tool 9 'Project navigator' if you're working on one chapter, or Tool 9 'Project navigator' followed by Tool 11 'Why our work matters' if you are working on two different chapters.
- If you are working on difficult topics that will challenge the team, consider starting with something easier and more positive to set a constructive mood before moving to a tougher task. For example, use Tool 10 'Define team purpose' before moving to Tool 20 'Conflict predictor'.

One-day workshop

- Three or four chapters with four tools maximum.
- Prep work for each team member will take 60 minutes before the session, either 30 minutes each for two different prep work tasks (and the other tools are done in the room without prep work), or 20 minutes each on three different tasks (leaving one for the session). This is because it's often unrealistic to ask people to do more than an hour of prep work.
- Consider which two tools will be best for the morning, often a positive one, then a challenging one, before doing another easier tool straight after lunch followed by a challenging one at the end of the day.

Five-day sprint

- Five chapters, one tool per chapter, or five tools from a few chapters.

- Monday to Friday at a set time each day (I suggest 9am to 11am before people get involved in other work).

- Before each session, assign a pre-read and prep task for the following day, and make sure people have booked time in their diaries to do both the prep work and the sessions.

- A possible supercharged teams sprint could look like this:

  - **Monday prep work:** Each person answers all the diagnostic questions in advance of the session in a Google sheet.

  - **Monday session:** Review the key themes and agree areas to work on for the other four days, assigning facilitators to each of the remaining four sessions.

  - **Monday actions:** Facilitators will choose which tools to use and design and send out the prep work tasks to be completed for the rest of the week,

  - **Tuesday:** The foundations of great teamwork, including prep work, session and actions.

  - **Wednesday:** Planning for success, including prep work, session and actions.

  - **Thursday:** How we behave together, including prep work, session and actions.

  - **Friday:** Increasing our chances of success, including prep work, session and actions.

To build team trust and keep things fair, don't leave it all up to one person to do the planning, facilitating or note-taking. Instead, ask different team members to be responsible for different roles and days, so you could assign one person to send and collate the prep work, another to facilitate on the day, and another to write up actions and outputs per day, rotating these so each team member has a role over the course of the project.

Like any great workshop, spend as much time planning for how to use the time as the session itself. The most important thing to remember is to make time as a team to use these tools on a regular basis – just as you would exercise regularly to maintain peak physical fitness.

A reminder of the 30 tools

Chapter 2: Choose your team

1: To team or not to team – do you really need a team?

2: Turning a group into a team – make a group of people into a team

3: Choose, avoid or separate – choose the right team members for your team

Chapter 3: Find more time

4: The timetable – measure where you spend your time and stop wasting it

5: Meeting sharpeners – make meetings shorter and sharper

6: Email agreement – set email etiquette to reduce time on email

Chapter 4: What goals do you want to achieve?

7: Five futures – define a successful vision of your project

8: Reframe your aim – make your team's objective more inspiring and ambitious

9: Project navigator – align on a project scope from the beginning

Chapter 5: Find your motivation

10: Define team purpose – why you are doing what you are doing

11: Why our work matters – create awareness of the positive impact of your work

12: Personal motivators – how you can benefit from your team's work

Chapter 6: Agree what you will deliver, and when

13: The journey plan – create a roadmap to your goal that includes the challenges you may face and milestones to track your progress

14: Accelerate and reflect – create a timeline that prioritises actions and includes time for reflection and refinement.

15: Measuring success checklist – plan to measure the success of your project outcomes, outputs and journey

Chapter 7: Ways to work together

16: Three-point check-in – build trust and develop empathy between team members

17: Our team rules – deliberately choose the team's rules of engagement

18: Distance culture code – set up the best ways of working if your team is in different locations

Chapter 8: Dealing with conflict

19: Opinions and instincts – identify disagreement and misalignment early on

20: Conflict predictor – predict the conflicts that might arise and avoid them

21: Six reasons why – learn from recent issues and prevent them from reoccurring

22: Individual intervention – address conflict with an individual in your team

Chapter 9: Get support from leaders

23: Direction of travel – understand your leaders' targets so you know if you're going in the right direction

24: Leader listening tool – really listen to your leader to develop true connection and understanding between you

25: Customer quiz – connect leaders with their customers

Chapter 10: Engage your stakeholders

26: Secret stakeholder survey – understand what your stakeholders think

27: Building session – get your stakeholders to build on the team's work

28: Start well, end well – start and end stakeholder meetings constructively

Chapter 11: Build a new culture

29: Code your culture – understand what people working in this culture do, and why

30: Create your culture – begin culture change with your team

Key take outs

- -

- The 30 tools are designed to be used in the day-to-day working life of your team.
- There are tools for all stages of your team journey.
- The 30 tools can be used to develop your team's strengths and develop areas for improvement.
- There's a supercharged teams workshop to suit all timeframes – from two hours to a five-day sprint.

Notes

Chapter 1

1. Loomes, V. (no date). The Future of Work. Two trends reshaping the future of work in 2020 and beyond! *TrendWatching*. Available from https://trendwatching.com/quarterly/the-future-of-work/the-future-of-work/ [Accessed 27 January 2020].

2. Kitching, J. (2016). *Exploring the UK Freelance Workforce in 2015*. Kingston-upon-Thames: IPSE. Available from https://www.ipse.co.uk/uploads/assets/uploaded/7d02d05b-8bc9-4bb5-926e8f39dd180ee8.pdf [Accessed 5 February 2020].

3. Mercer (2019). *Global talent trends 2019: Connectivity in the human age*. Available from https://www.mercer.com/content/dam/mercer/attachments/private/gl-2019-global-talent-trends-study.pdf [Accessed 17 April 2020].

4. Timewise (2019). *The Timewise Flexible Jobs Index 2019*. Available from https://timewise.co.uk/wp-content/uploads/2019/09/TW_Flexible_Jobs_Index_2019.pdf [Accessed 24 September 2019].

5. Edgar Pierce Professor of Social and Organizational Psychology, Harvard University (Coutu, 2009) Coutu, D. (2009). Why Teams Don't Work. *Harvard Business Review*. Available from https://hbr.org/2009/05/why-teams-dont-work [Accessed 12 November

6. Woolley, A.W., Chabris, C.F., Pentland, A., Hashmi, N. and Malone, T.W. (2010). Evidence for a Collective Intelligence Factor in the Performance of Human Groups. *Science*, 330 (6004), 686–88. Available from https://science.sciencemag.org/content/330/6004/686 [Accessed 12 November 2019].

7. Cross, R., Rebele, A and Grant, A. (2016). Collaboration Overload. *Harvard Business Review*. Available from https://hbr.org/2016/01/collaborative-overload [Accessed 12 November 2019].

8. MIT Human Resources (no date). The Basics of Working on Teams. *MIT Human Resources*. Available from https://hr.mit.edu/learning-topics/teams/articles/basics [Accessed 12 November 2019].

9. Co-founder of LinkedIn

10. Syed, M. (2020). Coronavirus: fixated on the flu and shrouded in secrecy, Britain's scientists picked the wrong remedy. *The Times*, 17 May. Available from https://www.thetimes.co.uk/article/coronavirus-fixated-on-the-flu-and-shrouded-in-secrecy-britains-scientists-picked-the-wrong-remedy-nmk8lsrr7?shareToken=0b4221a717040d8b97ac5a73f8bc2471 [Accessed 20 May 2020].

11. Skybrary (2016). Crew Resource Management (CRM). *Skybrary*. Available from https://www.skybrary.aero/index.php/Crew_Resource_Management_(CRM) [Accessed 20 May 2020].

12. Humphreys, G. (2008). Checklists save lives. *Bulletin of the World Health Organisation*, 86 (7), 497–576. Available from https://www.who.int/bulletin/volumes/86/7/08-010708/en/ [Accessed 20 May 2020].

13. Haynes, A.B. et al. (2009). A Surgical Safety Checklist to Reduce Morbidity and Mortality in a Global Population. *The New England Journal of Medicine*, 360 (5), 491–99. Available from https://www.who.int/patientsafety/safesurgery/Surgical_Safety_Checklist.pdf [Accessed 20 May 2020].

Chapter 2

1. Edgar Pierce Professor of Social and Organizational Psychology, Harvard University (Coutu, 2009)

2. MIT Human Resources (no date). Important steps when building a new team. Available from https://hr.mit.edu/learning-topics/teams/articles/new-team [Accessed 18 November 2019].

3. Sims, R.R. (1992). Linking Groupthink to Unethical Behavior in Organizations. *Journal of Business Ethics*, 11 (9), 651–62. Available from https://www.jstor.org/stable/25072319?mag=how-to-cure-groupthink&seq=1#metadata_info_tab_contents [Accessed 28 January 2020].

4. Levine, S. S., Apfelbaum, E. P., Bernard, M., Bartelt, V. L., Zajac, E. J., & Stark, D. (2014). Ethnic diversity deflates price bubbles. *Proceedings of the National Academy of Sciences of the United States of America*, 111 (52), 18524–9. Available from https://www.pnas.org/content/111/52/18524 [Accessed 28 January 2020].

5. In *The Human Edge*

6. writer and philosopher

7. Katzenbach, J.R. and Smith, D.K. (1993). *The Wisdom of Teams*. McGraw-Hill

8. Mathieu, J., Maynard, T. M., Rapp, T., & Gilson, L. (2008). Team effectiveness 1997–2007: A review of recent advancements and a glimpse into the future. *Journal of Management,* 34, 410-476.

9. Aubé, C. and Rousseau, V. (2011), Interpersonal aggression and team effectiveness: The mediating role of team goal commitment. *Journal of Occupational and Organizational Psychology*, 84 (3), 565–80.

Chapter 3

1. Hobsbawm, J. (2017). *Fully Connected: Social Health in an Age of Overload*. London: Bloomsbury.

2. Neeru Paharia and Anat Keinan, in *Conspicuous Consumption of Time: When Busynes and Lack of Leisure Time Become a Status Symbol*

3. Workfront (2019). The State of Work 2018–2019 U.S. Edition. Available from https://www.workfront.com/sites/default/files/files/2018-09/Report_2018-2019-State-of-Work-report-FINAL.pdf [Accessed 19 September 2019].

4. In Ferriss, T. (2007). *The 4-Hour Work Week: Escape 9–5, Live Anywhere and Join the New Rich.* Crown Business.

5. Ellson, A. (2019). Sorry, I'm in a meeting . . . for half of every working week. The Times, 19 August. Available from https://www.thetimes.co.uk/article/sorry-im-in-a-meeting-for-half-of-every-working-week-3c9gnwpnd [Accessed 19 September 2019].

Chapter 4

1. Ferguson, T. (2020). Outputs and outcomes: The two sides of workshop results. *Workshops.work*. Available from https://workshops.work/podcast/047/ [Accessed 28 February 2020].

2. Clarey, C. (2014). Olympians Use Imagery as Mental Training. *The New York Times*, 22 February. Available from https://www.nytimes.com/2014/02/23/sports/olympics/olympians-use-imagery-as-mental-training.html [Accessed 25 February 2020].

3. Adams, A.J. (2009). Seeing Is Believing: The Power of Visualization. *Psychology Today*, 3 December. Available from https://www.psychologytoday.com/us/blog/flourish/200912/seeing-is-believing-the-power-visualization [Accessed 25 February 2020]. Cohen, P. (2001). Mental gymnastics increase bicep strength. *New Scientist*, 21 November. Available from https://www.newscientist.com/article/dn1591-mental-gymnastics-increase-bicep-strength/ [Accessed 25 February 2020].

4. Busch, B. (2017). Research every teacher should know: setting expectations. *The Guardian*, 10 November. Available from https://www.theguardian.com/teacher-network/2017/nov/10/what-every-teacher-should-know-about-expectations [Accessed 25 February 2020]. Livingstone, J.S. (2003). Pygmalion in Management. *Harvard Business Review*, January. Available from https://hbr.org/2003/01/pygmalion-in-management [Accessed 25 February 2020].

5. Salo, O. (2017). How to create an agile organization. *McKinsey & Company*. Available from https://www.mckinsey.com/business-functions/organization/our-insights/how-to-create-an-agile-organization [Accessed 25 February 2020].

6. re:Work (no date). Guide: Understand team effectiveness. Available from https://rework.withgoogle.com/print/guides/5721312655835136/ [Accessed 3 February 2020]. Locke, E.A. and Latham, G.P. (2002). Building a practically useful theory of goal setting and task motivation – a 35 year odyssey. *American Psychologist*, 57 (9), 705–17. Available from https://www.researchgate.net/publication/11152729_Building_a_practically_useful_theory_of_goal_setting_and_task_motivation_-_A_35-year_odyssey [Accessed 25 February 2020].

7. NCVO (2019). *Time Well Spent: a national survey on the volunteer experience*. Available from https://www.ncvo.org.uk/images/documents/policy_and_research/volunteering/Volunteer-experience_Full-Report.pdf [Accessed 28 February 2020].

8. Captain of Moonshots, X

9. Rouse, M. (no date). Moonshot. *WhatIs*. Available from https://whatis.techtarget.com/definition/moonshot [Accessed 28 February 2020].

10. Selis, B., Lieb, R. and Szymanski, J. (2014). *The 2014 State of Digital Transformation: How Companies Are Investing in the Customer Digital Experience*. Altimeter. Available

from https://www.prophet.com/download/state-digital-transformation-2014/ [Accessed 28 February 2020].

11. Dörner, K. and Edelman, D. (2015). What 'digital' really means. *McKinsey & Company*. Available from https://www.mckinsey.com/industries/technology-media-and-telecommunications/our-insights/what-digital-really-means [Accessed 28 February 2020].

12. Selis, B., Lieb, R. and Szymanski, J. (2014). *The 2014 State of Digital Transformation: How Companies Are Investing in the Customer Digital Experience*. Altimeter. Available from https://www.prophet.com/download/state-digital-transformation-2014/ [Accessed 28 February 2020].

Chapter 5

1. Mercer (2019). *Global talent trends 2019: Connectivity in the human age*. Available from https://www.mercer.com/content/dam/mercer/attachments/private/gl-2019-global-talent-trends-study.pdf [Accessed 17 April 2020].

2. TrendWatching (no date). The Future of Purpose. Available from https://trendwatching.com/quarterly/2020-02/the-future-of-purpose/ [Accessed 17 April 2020].

3. re:Work (no date). KPMG: Motivating Employees Through a Deeper Sense of Purpose. Available from https://rework.withgoogle.com/case-studies/KPMG-purpose/ [Accessed 17 April 2020].

4. Bloomberg (2020). Bloomberg Gender-Equality Index. Available from https://data.bloomberglp.com/company/sites/46/2020/01/2020-MemberList.pdf [Accessed 17 April 2020].

5. Refinitiv (2019). Refinitiv Global Diversity and Inclusion Index. Available from https://www.refinitiv.com/content/dam/marketing/en_us/documents/reports/diversity-and-inclusion-top-100-companies.pdf [Accessed 17 April 2020].

6. Equileap (2019). Gender equality global report and ranking. Available from https://info.equileap.org/2019genderequality globalreportandranking [Accessed 17 April 2020].

7. Geena Davis Institute on Gender in Media and J. Walter Thompson (2017). Gender bias in advertising: research, trends and new visual language. *See Jane*. Available from https://seejane.org/research-informs-empowers/ gender-bias-advertising/ [Accessed 17 April 2020].

8. In *The Future of Work*

9. In *What is the Future of Work?*

10. ScienceDaily (2017). 'Purposeful leaders' are winning hearts and minds in workplaces, study finds. *ScienceDaily*, 14 June. Available from https://www.sciencedaily.com/ releases/2017/06/170614112908.htm [Accessed 17 April 2020].

11. Brower, T. (2019). Want to Find Your Purpose at Work? Change Your Perceptions. *Forbes*, 12 August. Available from https:// www.forbes.com/sites/tracybrower/2019/08/12/want-to-find-your-purpose-at-work-change-your-perceptions/#706345c01f48 [Accessed 17 April 2020].

12. Entrepreneur. Millar, B. (2020). How Sushi Daily founder Kelly Choi came back from the brink. *The Times*, 16 May. Available from https://www.thetimes.co.uk/article/kelly-choi-sushi-daily-net-worth-nfpcc8vn5?shareToken=385ad65dec10ced9 e2a6398851148716 [Accessed 20 May 2020].

13. Taylor, S. (2013). The Power of Purpose: Why is a sense of purpose so essential to our well-being? *Psychology Today*, 21 July. Available from https://www.psychologytoday.com/us/ blog/out-the-darkness/201307/the-power-purpose [Accessed 17 April 2020].

14. Hill, P.L. and Turiano, N.A. (2014). Purpose in Life as a Predictor of Mortality Across Adulthood. *Psychological Science*, 25 (7), 1482–6. Available from https://journals.sagepub.com/doi/ abs/10.1177/0956797614531799 [Accessed 17 April 2020].

15. In *The Infinite Game*

Chapter 6

1. Daily Mail Reporter. (2010). Bungling sailor used a road map to circumnavigate the UK . . . and ended up sailing round Isle of Sheppey for 36 hours. *Daily Mail*, 28 April. Available from https://www.dailymail.co.uk/news/article-1269257/Man-sailing-round-UK-using-road-map-circling-Isle-Sheppey-Kent-coast.html [Accessed 1 May 2020].

2. Grove, A. (1995). *High Output Management*. Vintage Books.

3. In *High Output Management*

4. Webb, C. (2016). *How to Have a Good Day: Harness the Power of Behavioural Science to Transform Your Working Life*. Penguin Random House USA. Citing Edwin A Locke and Gary P Latham

5. Castro, F. (no date). What is OKR? *Felipe Castro*. Available from https://felipecastro.com/en/okr/what-is-okr/ [Accessed 1 May 2020].

6. Former Commander of the International Space Station. Shah, V. (2018). A Conversation with Chris Hadfield, Former Commander of the International Space Station (ISS). *Thought Economics*, 26 November. Available from https://thoughteconomics.com/chris-hadfield/ [Accessed 6 May 2020].

7. Myles, R. (actor-writer-director) and Peachey, S. (actor-producer) (2020). The Show Must Go Online. *Rob Myles*. Available from https://robmyles.co.uk/theshowmustgoonline/ [Accessed 7 May 2020].

8. Skybrary (2016). Press-on-itis. *Skybrary*. Available from https://www.skybrary.aero/index.php/Press-on-itis_(OGHFA_BN) [Accessed 13 January 2020].

9. Innovation Leader and KPMG (2019). *Benchmarking Innovation Impact 2020*. Available from https://info.kpmg.us/content/dam/info/en/innovation-enterprise-solutions/pdf/2019/benchmarking-innovation-impact-2020.pdf [Accessed 3 May 2020].

10. 2020

11. Lim, S. (2020). Thai Airways rewards members air miles for staying at home. *The Drum*, 27 April. Available from https://www.thedrum.com/news/2020/04/27/thai-airways-rewards-members-airmiles-staying-home [Accessed 1 May 2020].

12. Atlassian Agile Coach (2019). What are sprints? *Atlassian Agile Coach*. Available from https://www.atlassian.com/agile/scrum/sprints [Accessed 5 November 2019].

13. In *The Innovator's Hypothesis*

14. Taneja, H. (2019). The Era of "Move Fast and Break Things" Is Over. *Harvard Business Review*. Available from https://hbr.org/2019/01/the-era-of-move-fast-and-break-things-is-over [Accessed 3 May 2020].

15. In *How to have a good day*

16. Singhal, R. (2016). Unintended consequences of demonetisation. *livemint,* 14 December. Available from https://www.livemint.com/Opinion/rpdrmaTifLZkmIvpDeVs0O/Unintended-consequences-of-demonetisation.html [Accessed 6 May 2020].

17. Quoted in *Team of Teams*. McChrystal, S. et al. (2015). *Team of Teams: New Rules of Engagement for a Complex World*. Penguin.

18. Ries, E. (2011). *The Lean Startup*. Crown Publishing Group. Agile Alliance (no date). Minimum Viable Product (MVP). *Agile Alliance*. Available from https://www.agilealliance.org/glossary/mvp/#q=~(infinite~false~filters~(tags~(~'mvp))~searchTerm~'~sort~false~sortDirection~'asc~page~1) [Accessed 3 May 2020].

19. Innovation Leader & KPMG, 2019

20. In *The Innovator's Hypothesis*

21. Scrum.org (no date). What is a sprint retrospective? Available from https://www.scrum.org/resources/what-is-a-sprint-retrospective [Accessed 6 May 2020].

Chapter 7

1. Atlassian (2019). Openness predicts a team's strength. Available from https://www.atlassian.com/open/research [Accessed 3 February 2020]. Sgroi, D. (2015). *Happiness and productivity: Understanding the happy-productive worker.* Social Market Foundation. Available from http://www.smf.co.uk/wp-content/uploads/2015/10/Social-Market-Foundation-Publication-Briefing-CAGE-4-Are-happy-workers-more-productive-281015.pdf#page=9 [Accessed 3 February 2020].

2. re:Work (no date). Set goals with OKRs. Available from https://rework.withgoogle.com/guides/set-goals-with-okrs/steps/introduction/ [Accessed 25 February 2020].

3. In *Smarter, faster, better: The Secrets of Productivity in life and business*

4. Schrage, M. (2019). The Age Of Average Is Over. *Futures in Focus.* Available from https://futuresinfocus.libsyn.com/guest-michael-schrage-2 [Accessed 13 January 2020].

5. Lewnes, A. (2020). I run a company of 230 people. How can I maintain a sense of community while working remotely? *The Sunday Times*, 3 May. Available from https://www.thetimes.co.uk/article/i-run-a-company-of-230-people-how-can-i-maintain-a-sense-of-community-while-working-remotely-mz60k6cx7 [Accessed 4 May 2020].

6. Duhigg, C. (2016). What Google Learned from Its Quest to Build the Perfect Team. *The New York Times*, 25 February. Available from https://www.nytimes.com/2016/02/28/magazine/what-google-learned-from-its-quest-to-build-the-perfect-team.html [Accessed 5 February 2020].

7. Founder of Millennial Mindset

Chapter 8

1. Chorley, M. (2019). Winds of change. *The Times*, 24 September. Available from https://www.thetimes.co.uk/article/winds-of-change-t76lbh6n8 [Accessed 21 April 2020].

2. In *The Culture Code*

3. Hill, L.A. et al. (2014). *Collective Genius: The art and practice of leading innovation*. Cambridge: Harvard Business Review Press.

4. In *Collective Genius*

5. Coyle, D. (2019). *The Culture Code: The secrets of highly successful groups*. Random House Business.

6. Ellis, R. (2020). Bosses cut staff absences by boosting wellbeing at work. *The Times*, 1 March. Available from https://www.thetimes.co.uk/article/bosses-cut-staff-absences-by-boosting-wellbeing-at-work-zlfdszrsx [Accessed 21 April 2020].

7. Hastings, R. (2009). Netflix Culture: Freedom & Responsibility. *SlideShare*. Available from https://www.slideshare.net/reed2001/culture-1798664 [Accessed 21 April 2020].

8. Fida, R. et al. (2018). 'First, Do No Harm': The Role of Negative Emotions and Moral Disengagement in Understanding the Relationship Between Workplace Aggression and Misbehavior. *Frontiers in Psychology*, 9, 671. Available from https://www.frontiersin.org/articles/10.3389/fpsyg.2018.00671/full [Accessed 21 April 2020].

Chapter 9

1. Innovation Leader & KPMG, 2019

2. Barta, T. and Barwise, P. (2017). Why effective leaders must manage up, down, and sideways. *McKinsey Quarterly*, 27 April.

Available from https://www.mckinsey.com/featured-insights/leadership/why-effective-leaders-must-manage-up-down-and-sideways [Accessed 9 May 2020].

3. Morgan, J. (2014). This is the Single Greatest Cause of Employee Disengagement. *Forbes*, 13 October. Available from https://www.forbes.com/sites/jacobmorgan/2014/10/13/this-is-the-single-greatest-cause-of-employee-disengagement/#2 85de9b82c57 [Accessed 9 May 2020].

4. Aghina, W. et al. (2018). The five trademarks of agile organizations. *McKinsey & Company*. Available from https://www.mckinsey.com/business-functions/organization/our-insights/the-five-trademarks-of-agile-organizations [Accessed 9 May 2020].

5. Nasdaq (2019). Nasdaq President & CEO: Re-think Nasdaq – We are a Global Technology Company. *Advisor Perspectives*. Available from https://www.advisorperspectives.com/videos/2019/06/01/nasdaq-president-ceo-rethink-nasdaq-we-are-a-global-technology-company [Accessed 9 May 2020].

6. Wirearchy (no date). What is wirearchy? Available from http://wirearchy.com/what-is-wirearchy/ [Accessed 9 May 2020].

7. Hastings, 2009

8. In *Measure what matters*

9. Etymonline (no date). Priority (n.). Available from https://www.etymonline.com/word/priority [Accessed 9 May 2020].

10. Mercier, D. (2018). The biggest mistakes managers make when managing millennials. *Medium*. Available from https://medium.com/pathlight/the-biggest-mistakes-managers-make-when-managing-millennials-ff849868bf8e [Accessed 9 May 2020].

11. Grow (no date). Metric Of The Week: North Star Metric. Available from https://www.grow.com/blog/what-is-a-north-star-metric [Accessed 9 May 2020].

12. Hegde, S. (2018). Every Product Needs a North Star Metric: Here's How to Find Yours. *Amplitude*. Available from https://amplitude.com/blog/2018/03/21/product-north-star-metric [Accessed 9 May 2020].

13. De Smet, A., Lurie, M. and St George, A. (2018). *Leading agile transformation: The new capabilities leaders need to build 21st Century organizations*. McKinsey & Company. Available from https://www.mckinsey.com/~/media/mckinsey/business%20functions/organization/our%20insights/leading%20agile%20transformation%20the%20new%20capabilities%20leaders%20need%20to%20build/leading-agile-transformation-the-new-capabilities-leaders-need-to-build-21st-century-organizations.ashx [Accessed 9 May 2020].

14. In *The Little Prince*

15. Hegde, S. (2018). The Three Games of Customer Engagement Strategy. *Amplitude*. Available from https://amplitude.com/blog/customer-engagement-strategy [Accessed 9 May 2020].

16. Stefan Homeister Leadership (2020). Available from https://stefan-homeister-leadership.com/?lang=en [Accessed 10 May 2020].

17. Grove, 1995.

18. Leitwolf (2019). Interview Paul Polman: The essence of successful leadership – trees and leaders. Available from https://leitwolf.libsyn.com/interview-paul-polman-the-essence-of-successful-leadership-trees-and-leaders [Accessed 9 May 2020].

19. Psychotherapist

20. In conversation

21. Greenleaf, R.K. (2002). *Servant Leadership: A Journey into the Nature of Legitimate Power and Greatness*, 25th anniversary edition. Paulist Press.

22. Bower, M. (1997). Developing leaders in business. *McKinsey Quarterly*. Available from https://www.mckinsey.com/

featured-insights/leadership/developing-leaders-in-a-business [Accessed 28 April 2020].

23. Leitwolf (2019).

24. van den Driest, F., Sthanunathan, S. and Weed, K. (2016). Building an Insights Engine. *Harvard Business Review.* Available from https://hbr.org/2016/09/building-an-insights-engine [Accessed 9 May 2020].

25. Delhoume, M. (2019). Why marketers must pursue creativity and excellence. *Raconteur,* 10 June. Available from www. raconteur.net/hr/marketers-creativity-excellence [Accessed 15 July 2020].

26. Founder and Executive Chairman, World Economic Forum. Vincent, M. (no date). A new paradigm requires new thinking. *Applied Change.* Available from https://appliedchange.co.uk/a-new-paradigm-requires-new-thinking/ [Accessed 9 May 2020].

27. Webb, C. (2016) *How to Have a Good Day: Harness the Power of Behavioural Science to Transform Your Working Life.* Penguin Random House USA. (citing Danziger, S., Levav, J. and Avnaim-Pesso, L. (2011). Extraneous factors in judicial decisions. *Proceedings of the National Academy of Sciences of the United States of America,* 108 (17), 6889–92. Available from https://www.pnas.org/content/pnas/108/17/6889.full.pdf [Accessed 9 May 2020])

28. Sasaki, T., Pratt, S.C. and Kacelnik, A. (2018). Parallel vs. comparative evaluation of alternative options by colonies and individuals of the ant Temnothorax rugatulus. *Scientific Reports,* 8 (1), 12730. Available from https://doi.org/10.1038/s41598-018-30656-7 [Accessed 9 May 2020].

29. Former Commander of the International Space Station. Shah, V. (2018). A Conversation with Chris Hadfield, Former Commander of the International Space Station (ISS). *Thought Economics,* 26 November. Available from https://thoughteconomics.com/chris-hadfield/ [Accessed 6 May 2020].

30. In *Building an Insights Engine*

Chapter 10

1. Clayton, M. (2014). *The Influence Agenda*. London: Palgrave Macmillan.

2. Cambridge Dictionary (no date). Not-invented-here syndrome. Available from https://dictionary.cambridge.org/dictionary/ english/not-invented-here-syndrome [Accessed 28 April 2020].

3. Innovation Leader & KPMG, 2019

4. Head of User Experience, Google Cloud (Innovation Leader & KPMG, 2019)

5. Advaney, M. (2017). To Talk or Not To Talk That Is The Question! *Youth Time Magazine*, 5 June. Available from https:// youth-time.eu/to-talk-or-not-to-talk-that-is-the-question-at-least-70-percent-of-communication-is-non-verbal/ [Accessed 28 April 2020].

6. Garbuio, M. and Lovallo, D. (2017). Does organizational politics kill company growth? *Review of International Business and Strategy*, 27 (4), 410–33. Available from https://doi. org/10.1108/RIBS-09-2017-0073 [Accessed 28 April 2020].

7. In *Bored and Brilliant*

8. In *On Leadership*

9. Basford, T. and Schaninger, B. (2016). The four building blocks of change. *McKinsey Quarterly*. Available from https:// www.mckinsey.com/business-functions/organization/ our-insights/the-four-building-blocks--of-change [Accessed 28 April 2020].

10. In *The Innovator's Hypothesis*

11. Founder of Lowercase Capital. Ferriss, T. (2016). *Tools of Titans: The Tactics, Routines, and Habits of Billionaires, Icons, and World-Class Performers*. Vermilion.

12. Edsel Bryant Ford Professor of Business Administration, Harvard Business School

13. Pfeffer, J. and Sutton, R.I. (1999). The Smart-Talk Trap. *Harvard Business Review*. Available from https://hbr.org/1999/05/the-smart-talk-trap [Accessed 7 May 2020].

Chapter 11

1. Heathfield, S.M. (2020). Culture: Your environment for people at work. *The Balance Careers*. Available from https://www.thebalancecareers.com/culture-your-environment-for-people-at-work-1918809 [Accessed 16 April 2020].

2. Innovation Leader & KPMG, 2019

3. Schein, E. (1984) Coming to a new awareness of organizational culture. Sloan Management Review 25 (2), 3–16. Available from https://sloanreview.mit.edu/article/coming-to-a-new-awareness-of-organizational-culture/ [Accessed 16 April 2020].

4. In *The Age of Average Is Over*

5. Chief Talent Officer, Netflix, 1998–2012

6. Moore, P. (2015). Pret a Manger – Behind the scenes at the 'Happy Factory'. *The Guardian*, 14 April. Available from https://www.theguardian.com/small-business-network/2015/apr/14/pret-a-manger-happy-coffee-chain#maincontent [Accessed 16 April 2020].

7. Blundell, J., Rosenbach, F., Hameed, T. and FitzGerald, C. (2019). *Are we rallying together? Collaboration and public sector reform*. Oxford: Government Outcomes Lab. Available from https://s3.eu-west-2.amazonaws.com/golab.prod/documents/BSG-GOLab-AreWeRallyingTogether.pdf [Accessed 16 April 2020].

8. in *The Culture Code*

9. Mercer (2019)

Chapter 12

1. National Research Council (1999). *The Changing Nature of Work: Implications for Occupational Analysis*. Washington DC: The National Academies Press. Available from https://www.nap.edu/catalog/9600/the-changing-nature-of-work-implications-for-occupational-analysis [Accessed 21 April 2020].

2. In *The Road Ahead*

3. Founder and Executive Chairman, World Economic Forum. Schwab, K. (2016). The Fourth Industrial Revolution: what it means, how to respond. *World Economic Forum*. Available from https://www.weforum.org/agenda/2016/01/the-fourth-industrial-revolution-what-it-means-and-how-to-respond/ [Accessed 27 January 2020].

4. In *The Human Edge*

5. PwC (2018). Workforce of the future – The competing forces shaping 2030. PwC. Available from https://www.pwc.com/gx/en/services/people-organisation/workforce-of-the-future/workforce-of-the-future-the-competing-forces-shaping-2030-pwc.pdf [Accessed 27 January 2020].

6. Ethical Consumer (2018). *Ethical Consumer Markets Report 2018*. Manchester: Ethical Consumer Research Association. Available from https://www.ethicalconsumer.org/sites/default/files/inline-files/EC%20Markets%20Report%202018%20FINAL.pdf [Accessed 27 January 2020].

7. TrendWatching (no date). Trend Framework. Available from https://premium.trendwatching.com/trend-framework/ [Accessed 27 January 2020].

8. Loomes

9. Smith, A. (2019). Microsoft Productivity Score: Insights that transform how work gets done. *Microsoft*. Available from https://techcommunity.microsoft.com/t5/microsoft-365-blog/

microsoft-productivity-score-insights-that-transform-how-work/ ba-p/969722 [Accessed 27 January 2020].

10. Mercer (2019)

11. In TrendWatching

12. Schrage (2019)

13. In *The Age of Average is Over*

14. Learning Theories (no date). Pareto Principle. Available from https://www.learning-theories.com/pareto-principle.html [Accessed 27 January 2020].

15. Trend-Watching

16. Group Head of Analytics and Artificial Intelligence, Axiata

17. Author

Index